A Handful of Zen

A Handful of Zen

by

by Camden Benares

FALCON PRESS

As of September 1, 1990 e.v., our new name will be:

NEW FALCON PUBLICATIONS

LAS VEGAS

International Standard Book Number: 0-941404-88-9

First Edition 1990 by Falcon Press

Book Design, Typography and Production by
RapidScribe Communications
A division of
Studio 31/Royal Type
27 West 20th Street • Room 1005
New York, NY 10011

Cover Painting by Jane Nelson
Cover Design by Studio 31

FALCON PRESS
1209 South Casino Center, Suite 147
Las Vegas, Nevada 89104
1-702-385-5749

Manufactured in the United States of America

DEDICATION

This book is dedicated to my wife, June Benares, whose love and support helped make it possible.

ACKNOWLEDGEMENT

The author thanks various Discordians for their permission to quote and misquote.

CONTENTS

CHAPTER 1

The First Sounds of Zen

Periodically in the West, an upsurge of interest in Zen occurs. Zen is mentioned in articles, fiction, comedy routines and conversation. The Zen stories told and the Zen questions asked can convince the listener or reader that there is something to Zen; but that something can seem maddeningly elusive and obscurely mystical. There is no system of mysticism inherent in Zen. Zen can be understood and demystified.

Zen is a combination of Buddhist and Taoist views and developed practices. Zen is a way of liberation, liberation from limiting belief systems and low consciousness thinking. As a journey of self-discovery, it guides the traveler into an expanded reality.

The direct flavor of Zen is neatly captured in the following traditional Zen story:

The Zen Monk's Burden

Two Zen monks came to a muddy street on their way to the monastery. A pretty young woman was standing on the corner, afraid she would dirty her best clothes if she crossed.

The first monk said, "I'll carry you" to the woman. She got on the monk's back and he carried her across the street.

The second monk didn't speak until they were in sight

Two monks saw a pretty young woman afraid of getting her best clothes dirty if she crossed the muddy street.

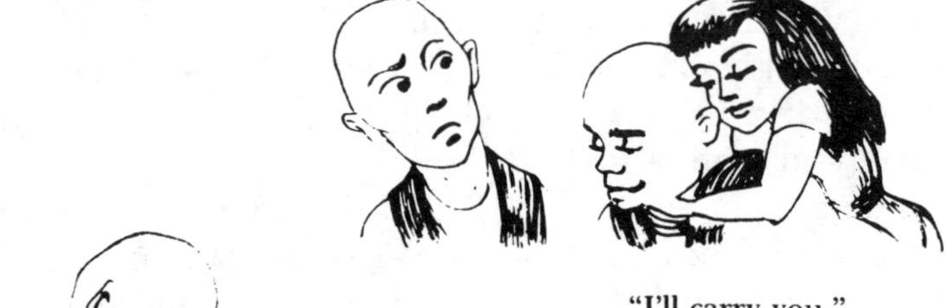

"I'll carry you."

The second monk said, "Monks shouldn't touch pretty young women. Why did you?"

"I put her down as soon as I got through the mud. You are still carrying her."

of the monastery. Then he said, "Monks shouldn't touch pretty young women. Why did you?"

The first monk replied, "I put her down as soon as I got through the mud. You are still carrying her."

That story reveals that the first monk has the spirit of Zen and that the second monk is burdened by his mistaking guides for gods. The first monk acted in the personal reality he was experiencing. The second monk is a victim of his belief system, locked into unpleasant and low consciousness thoughts about a situation that has been resolved everywhere except in his own mind.

Modern Zen stories often deal with Zen-oriented people in their everyday actions in the West, in a life far removed from the setting of a monastery or retreat. The following modern Zen story deals with the combination of two problems in the West—divorce and attachment to material possessions:

Joint Property

A couple who had decided to divorce consulted a Zen-oriented family counselor for help in dividing their possessions. Their problem was a few jointly owned items that both wanted. They gave the counselor a list of the material things that needed to be divided between them. The counselor looked at the list, handed it back, and said to the person who took it, "Divide these goods into two piles of approximately equal value." The counselor then turned to the other member of the couple and said, "After the division is made, you choose which pile you want."

The counselor got both people to accept half of their joint property in a way that did not pit them against each other. He solved the problem by enabling both people to operate in their individual self-interest without making a victim of the former partner. Zen can act like scissors to cut the red tape of life.

Zen places an emphasis on learning from individual experience. This is often best done by total identification with the experience. Such unity, where there is no separation between the experience and the person who is experiencing, adds the Zen essence to learning. The following story relates how one Japanese Zen Master began to teach one person such unity:

The Student of Swords

A young man who wanted to be the best swordsman in Japan went to see the Zen Master who was reputed to be the best teacher of swordsmanship. He told the Zen Master that he would become the Zen Master's servant if accepted as a student. He then asked the Zen Master how long it would take for him to become a swordsman.

"Five years," was the reply.

"But if I work twice as hard as any other student," asked the young man, "how long will it take me then?"

"Ten years," said the Zen Master. "Hurrying slows down learning."

The young man accepted that and asked, "Will you take me as a student?"

"No," said the Zen Master, "but if you promise not to mention swords or touch a sword or talk of swordsmanship, I will accept you as my servant."

The young man worked hard as a servant, longing to be a student. After months passed, one day the Zen Master in passing administered a hard blow to his servant's back with the staff he carried. The young man realized he was being taught but he was not sure what the lesson was.

During the days that followed, the Zen Master continued his surprise attacks. The young man, thinking that he was being taught to be quick, became an artful dodger but his back remained sore from the Zen Master's blows.

One day the Zen Master struck his servant's back with his staff while the servant was scrubbing the floor. The young man made no move to protect himself and continued his work. The Zen Master said, "You have learned that there is no way to protect yourself from a surprise attack from the rear. You may move into the student quarters."

The student mastered his lessons and became a swordsman of great repute.

Of course the Zen Master could have told the student during their first meeting that there is no defense for a surprise attack from the rear. That would merely have given the student some knowledge. For the knowledge to be useful in swordsmanship, it had to be part of the student's personal experience.

The same kind of learning from individual experience is the subject of this western Zen story:

The Busboy

After the last customer left the restaurant, a busboy asked the manager if he could be promoted to waiter. The manager had just finished erasing the blackboard listing the dinner specialities for that evening; she asked the busboy, "What were the dinner specialities tonight?" The busboy didn't know. The manager said, "When you know things like that because you want to know them, ask me again about becoming a waiter."

That story emphasized the importance of getting the most out of personal experience. If the busboy pays attention to his experience he may become a superb waiter or he may learn that he should try another business. Either choice, based on knowledge of the self, is the way of Zen.

Zen questions like "What is the sound of one hand clapping?" defy any logical answer. A Zen question isn't a joke or a riddle but a puzzle designed to increase intuition, to illustrate the limits of logic, to show the boundaries of words, to challenge the mind to discover the self.

The answer, or any answer, to a Zen question is not important in itself. What is important is the process that the person goes through seeking the answer. That process produces valuable self-knowledge. That process can bring an intuitive understanding of the relationship between the question and the answer.

Although a few of the traditional Zen questions are heard in the West today, there are some modern Zen questions designed to achieve the goals of liberation. Here are several:

"Will the illusions you choose not to lose bring you joy?"

"Who is the you that is doing things that are not in your intelligent self-interest?"

"If you can't be yourself, who can you be?"

"If you aren't here now, are you nowhere?"

"Why do you expect more of yourself than you expect of others?"

"Why do you expect more of others than you expect of yourself?"

The traditional Zen questions are used in the master-student relationship. The Zen Master aids the process the student experiences by rejecting unsatisfactory answers until the student has a breakthrough of understanding. Modern Zen questions are obviously aimed toward self-knowledge; the difference is that the Zen practitioner must find individual answers that are personally satisfactory. The search for an answer can be as difficult as verbalizing the sound of one hand clapping—one answer to "What is the sound of one hand clapping?" is a handful of Zen.

EXERCISES—NOT FOR EVERYONE

These exercises are not for everyone. Readers who seek only a verbal understanding of Zen should skip the exercises and read the next chapter. The reader who seeks the benefits of Zen should read the exercises carefully and perform any or all of them at an appropriate time and place. Any of the exercises in this book may be repeated as needed or abandoned if found unsatisfactory. Some of the exercises may take some time; there is no need for hurry. The exercises should not be allowed to interfere with the reading of the rest of the book.

1. The Zen Journal Exercise

The reader who wants Zen experiences should start a personal Zen journal. Date each entry. The first entry could start: "I am learning about Zen because . . ." Write in the journal those things that are important to you rather than those things you might think others would find interesting about Zen or about you. Write down the important questions in your life that you hope to resolve through

Zen or other means. Some of the questions you write will be answered; other questions will fade from importance as you gain the experience necessary to ask the right questions. Your Zen journal will track your own development.

2. The Burden Exercise

In the first Zen story in this chapter, The Zen Monk's Burden, the second monk is carrying the mental burden that is a hindrance to him. He cannot change the past and he must come to terms with it before he can put down his heavy burden. If there is something like that burden in your mind, something that relates only to the past and is only a handicap in the present and future, write down on paper a few words to symbolize your burden. Examine that paper and see it as the burden you have carried. Throw the paper in your trash. Take out your trash.

3. The Possessions Exercise

The emphasis on material goods in Western cultures can create an automatic response of attachment to goods. Once those goods have no functional, decorative or emotional value, they are merely clutter. Anytime you can give something you have but don't want to someone who wants it, you improve two realities—your personal reality and the personal reality of someone else. Examine the good feeling you get from this action. Write your thoughts about it in your journal.

4. The Attention Exercise

The busboy didn't immediately get a waiter's position because he hadn't paid attention to his experience. Each life produces a wealth of experience about living. Start keeping your attention on your experience to make the business of living easier. If you find certain experience positive, pay attention to what created the positive feelings. If you find certain experiences negative, examine closely the personal thoughts that identified the experience as negative. Most experience is neutral until thought about. You can change your thinking and you can change your experience.

5. Questioning Exercise

Select one of the Zen questions as your question. Write that question in your journal along with any answers that occur to you. When you feel like thinking, think about other possible answers and add them to your journal.

CHAPTER 2

Buddhist Roots

Zen is concerned with experience. As a way of liberation, Zen directs the follower through higher levels of consciousness toward the experience of enlightenment. This overwhelming sense of sudden, great awakening was the great achievement of the human being who became known as Buddha, a name meaning the enlightened one.

He was born into a wealthy and privileged Hindu family in north-eastern India more than 2500 years ago. He was named Siddhartha Gautama. His life was one of sensuous luxury where his desires were encouraged and satisfied. His father discouraged Siddhartha from leaving his palace and estate because he wanted to protect his son from any sad or harsh experiences.

Siddhartha yearned to know more of the world. Eventually he persuaded his father to let him journey to the capital with a driver for the horse-drawn chariot. On this trip, Siddhartha had the driver explain to him three things that he saw for the first time: old age, sickness, and death.

He was shocked and disturbed to learn that all human beings were susceptible to these forces. He was overwhelmed by the insecurity of life, realizing that joy and pleasure could suddenly change to frustration and suffering. His values and beliefs were overturned. He knew that he could no longer lead the life he had led. His existence seemed futile. He longed for a deeper reality.

At this time, there was no concept of Hinduism as a religion. The Hindu way of life was an orally transmitted body of tradition that dealt with every aspect of daily life

Siddhartha yearned to know more of the world. Eventually he persuaded his father to let him journey to the capital with a driver for the horse-drawn chariot.

from the mundane to the divine. The Hindu caste system was a rigid social order that resisted all change at every level.

Siddhartha Gautama took the only path he saw available that could lead him to a deeper reality; he abandoned the life of convention and embraced the casteless, homeless life of the seeker of liberation. This action was in keeping with Hindu traditions. A person who wanted change either opted for a life outside society or the social order would push that individual to the very bottom of society.

Siddhartha Gautama rejected the privileged life because he had seen that its rewards and values could not protect him from the frustration and suffering of old age, sickness, and death. He left his position of power because it did not give him the answers he needed to the questions about the human condition that preoccupied him.

For seven years, Siddhartha Gautama continued his search for the truths that would ease and end human frustration and suffering. He found no teacher with the answers he sought. Eventually he joined a band of ascetics who lived an austere life in the jungle. They strived to subdue their passions through stringent self-discipline and hardship.

The five ascetics accepted Gautama as one of their band. They admired the will with which he trained his mind and body to accept adversity. Soon they regarded him as their leader but he still felt he hadn't found the answers he was seeking.

Although many people sought his blessing because of his reputed holiness, Gautama continued his own search. His frequent fasting left him weak, emaciated, unable to think clearly. He decided to resume eating. His five disciples left him, believing that he had abandoned his goals.

Gautama sat under a tree to meditate. There he had the experience of enlightenment, of complete awakening. This experience is central to Zen; this is the experience to which Zen points. Gautama had found the spiritual illumination that he had been seeking. He had become the Buddha.

When Buddha was ready to teach, he went to the Deer Park near the city of Benares, also called Varanasi. There he found the five disciples who had left him earlier. He told them of his enlightenment, overcame their skepticism and revealed his doctrine. Buddha gave this doctrine a numerical orientation so it could be easily remembered and spread by oral teaching. This teaching is called the four noble truths and the eightfold path.

The first noble truth is the existence of frustration and suffering. Being in contact with that which is not liked causes frustration and suffering just as being separated from that which is desired.

The second noble truth is that frustration and suffering are caused by clinging, clutching and grasping based on ignorance and the lack of self-knowledge. Such actions are like the hand trying to grasp itself or the body trying to outrun its shadow.

The third noble truth is that frustration and suffering can be ended. They can be ended when there is enough self-knowledge to transcend clinging, clutching and grasping.

The fourth noble truth is that the way to end frustration and suffering is to follow the eightfold path. The eightfold path consists of:

1. Complete views
2. Right intentions
3. Truthful speech
4. Correct conduct
5. Appropriate vocation
6. Earnest effort
7. Continuing alertness
8. Thorough concentration

Complete views consist of seeing the world as it is and seeing the self as it is. Right intentions are based on these views and are guides to behavior that minimize frustration and suffering for the self and for others. The next five numbers on the path deal with action; they emphasize behavior intended to help an individual interact with the world and others without creating frustration and suffering. Thorough concentration on the actions and the results of action provides more information on complete views, the first item on the path.

The eightfold path is a feedback system that guides an individual toward enlightenment by basing action on direct experience. Each action leads to more knowledge. Each bit of knowledge is used as a guide to further experience. As experience changes an individual's thoughts change. These changes have the effect of changing the perceived world because each individual exists in a personal reality that is created by what a person thinks about his or her own experience.

Buddha taught the doctrine of the four noble truths and the eightfold path until his death, about 50 years after his enlightenment. He had wrestled with the problem of human suffering and found a solution that he believed was universal; he devoted his life to sharing that solution with all who were interested.

Enlightenment, the complete awakening of the individual, is the key experience of Zen. Many Zen stories give details about what occurred prior to the enlightenment of a person. Such stories often leave the reader with the feeling that you had to be there to appreciate it fully. Other Zen stories, like the following one, reveal that life is still lived in an ordinary manner after enlightenment:

Before and After Enlightenment

A student who observed the Zen Master moving through life as effortlessly as a boat travelling with the current asked, "What was your life like before you became enlightened?"

The Zen Master replied, "I ate, drank, worked, rested and slept."

"And since your enlightenment?" asked the student.

"I eat when hungry, drink when thirsty, work when work needs doing, rest when tired, and sleep when my day is over."

The product of Buddha's enlightenment is his doctrine of the four noble truths and the eightfold path. It is not a theological doctrine—there is no mention of any deities and therefore no conflict with any theological theory. Buddha presented himself as a human being, not a god, who had discovered some ultimate truth he wished to share with others. He perceived the universe as a unity encompassing all that exists.

The eightfold path is a guide to individual behavior and the individual raising of consciousness. It doesn't specify the rights of others or define morality but those who are concerned with rights and morals have no quarrel with Buddha's doctrine. A modern Zen story points to the popularity of Buddha's path:

Sam's Choice

When asked why he became a Buddhist, Sam said, "for years I suffered whenever reality didn't match my expectations. I got very good at denial and convinced almost everyone that I wasn't suffering but I couldn't convince myself.

"I next looked at suffering as if it were an illusion and not a reality. My struggles with that concept convinced me that even if suffering is an illusion, it is a very painful illusion and the experience is real to the person who is suffering.

"The I took the position that since suffering exists and is apparently universal, there must be a value in it that I hadn't recognized. I though about it and developed a model of reality in which suffering was essential for individual creativity, for achievement, for growth and for learning. What I learned from my suffering was that it wasn't good for me.

"Once I recognized that I needed to stop suffering, I began investigating how others had dealt with suffering. Buddha seemed to be the only teacher who presented a method that made sense to me and didn't require me to review and relive all the suffering I had already gone through. I saw the eightfold path as something worth trying even though I considered it highly optimistic. I started following the path and discovered that most of my suffering disappeared as my thinking about it changed."

OPTIONAL EXERCISES

1. Journal Entry

Copy the four noble truths and the eightfold path into your Zen journal. Write down what you think about them now. Later you can reread these thoughts and examine how a change in thought creates a change in experience.

2. Seeing and Walking the Path

Make several copies of the eightfold path. Post them where you will see them often. Take one copy with you for an eight-block walk. Let each block represent in your mind one step of the path. Look for the reality of that step within that block.

3. Answering Exercise

Whenever you are unable to find an answer that is stored in your memory, don't frustrate yourself by continuing to demand that the information come forward immediately if you don't need it immediately. Mentally, ask the question like this: "Answer Department, I would like the answer to the following question as soon as you can find it: Where did I put the . . .?" Repeat the question. Then go on to the next thing. Easing the pressure is as apt to produce the answer as any other procedure.

4. Pressure Reducing Exercise

If you had success with the previous exercise, adapt it to some of the other demands you place on yourself that cause frustration and suffering.

5. Good Deed Exercise

Whenever you feel frustrated, make an effort to reduce the frustration that someone else is experiencing. Perform this good deed without calling attention to yourself. Pay attention to the good feelings this creates in you. Write how you feel in your journal. Notice that you feel better about yourself after doing a good deed even if no one else knows you did it. Recognize that this good feeling is not dependent on the thoughts, beliefs, actions or the personal realities of others.

CHAPTER 3

Taoist Trunks

When Buddhist missionaries from India entered China many centuries after Buddha's death, they encountered Taoism (pronounced dowism), a spiritual and religious philosophy concerned with the observation of nature and the discovery of nature's way. Tao means the way of nature or the path of nature.

Taoists see the overall pattern of nature as Tao, the system that contains all other systems, the ecology of all existence. Tao is the flow of what happens, not a set of laws or rules that are enforced. Each action becomes part of the Tao as it happens because every act is connected to everything else.

Taoists perceive all that exists as a moving unity, the Tao—which is not made up of parts just as the human body is not assembled from parts. the names given to specific areas do not separate these areas from the whole in the Taoist view.

Taoism focuses on the cyclic aspects of nature. The continuing movement of water is a prime example familiar to Westerners. Water vapor in the air condenses to form clouds. Clouds release the water as precipitation, rain that falls to earth. Eventually the water evaporates to form water vapor and the cycle of condensation, precipitation, and evaporation repeats.

The Taoist observes nature knowing that the observer and the observations are not separate from what is being observed. The observations are not motivated by a desire to conquer, change, or quantify nature but to see the way of existing in harmony with nature. This is not a matter of faith or trust in nature but a recognition that the processes of nature and the processes of the individual are the same thing, manifestations of the Tao, the way of nature. Examples of Taoist harmony in action are swimming with the current and sailing with the wind.

The symbol of Taoism is the circular image of yin and yang together as polarities in harmony. The original meaning of yin was the shady side of a mountain; yang meant the sunny side of a mountain. In the symbol, the light dot in the dark area represents the yang in yin: the dark dot in the light area represents the yin in yang. The symbol has a rotational symmetry that represents the cyclic movement of natural processes.

Yin and yang represent the archetypal poles of nature such as dark and light, female and male, winter and summer. These poles are not in conflict. They are like head and tails of a coin or the north and south poles of a magnet; one does not exist without the other—together they represent unity and harmony. The dot of yang in yin and of yin in yang symbolizes the idea that when one energy of nature reaches an extreme, the other energy is within it ready for a new cycle. Taoists see nature as a cyclic process of transformation and change. The Taoist ideal is to live in harmony with this process, simply and naturally. From the Taoist viewpoint, any action aimed at eliminating either of the complementary forces within nature is based on not understanding nature.

The Taoist concept of the unity of opposites is readily understood in examples like the two sides of a coin and the two poles of a magnet. For those who think that opposites are in conflict, this can be a difficult concept. If a student of Taoism believes that there is a constant struggle of life versus death, the Taoist teacher has to

The symbol of Taoism is the circular image of yin and yang together as polarities in harmony.

bring the student to the realization that life and death work in harmony. Neither exists without the other. Continued life is made possible only by the death of whatever the living consume regardless of whether it is plant or animal. When the living die, they are consumed or they decay to foster life and the continuation of the cycle.

One Taoist teacher taught her student about the unity of opposites with the following experience:

The Path

> A Taoist teacher asked her student to accompany her on a hike. The teacher, with her student at her side, walked to the foot of a small mountain and started up the path that led to the top. About halfway up, she stopped and asked her student, "Which way is up?" He pointed up. She asked, "Which way is down?" He pointed down. She said, "The same path takes you up and down. That is the unity of opposites. If you again tell me that you don't understand the unity of opposites, I will tell you to take a hike."

Taoists recognize that conflict exists within sections of the patterns of nature, but they have the concept of mutually arising harmony among the many patterns of nature that are mutually dependent on each other. One expression of the mutually arising harmony in Taoist teachings is that the universe forms consciousness and consciousness evokes the universe. This is an ancient way of saying that a person's personal reality is created by the thoughts of that person's consciousness.

Taoists see cause and effect as a too narrow focus on reality, a viewpoint that misses most of the pattern. To a Taoist, cause and effect are just two fish caught in the net of the mind. A Taoist musician once explained it this way:

"Cause and effect are two notes of one song, not enough to give you the rhythm or the melody. I can blow into this horn and make an E flat note come out. Of course E flat won't come out if I don't blow it but that's not simple cause and effect. If I blow and don't finger the valves correctly there will be no E flat. If the valves don't work right or if the horn is clogged, there'll be no E flat. If I don't want to blow E flat, I can blow another note. People who can't get beyond cause and effect miss the rhythms and melodies of life."

Taoists are observers of nature but they are not nature worshipers because they perceive everything that exists as natural. The Taoist sees his house as being as natural as a bird's nest or an animal's den. Taoism conceives of no creator separate from something created because all is Tao. The Taoist's ideal of harmony with nature consists of acting spontaneously in accordance with one's true nature by trusting one's innate, intuitive intelligence.

The Taoist concept of the relativity of all values can be shown in the following modern Zen story that parallels older Taoist tales:

Who Knows?

Eric's son became a star on his high school football team. Eric's neighbor congratulated him on his son's achievement by saying how good the situation was.

Eric said, "Who knows what's good and what's bad?"

The neighbor replied, "But he will probably get a college scholarship. Wouldn't that be great?"

Eric knew that his son had never expressed an interest in college. He answered, "Who knows what's good and what's bad?"

Eric's son injured his knee permanently in a football

game and was told that he would never be able to play football again. Eric's neighbor said, "I think it's just terrible that your son has a bum knee."

Eric responded. "Who knows what's good and what's bad?"

When a war started, the draft board called Eric's son. Eric's son was not drafted because of his damaged knee. Eric's neighbor decided not to judge the situation.

There was no conflict between Chinese Taoism and Indian Buddhism. Both were focused on practical means for living a harmonious life. Neither required belief in any theological system. They blended into the way of liberation known as Chan. Chan means meditation leading to insight.

Chan Buddhism became one of the major schools of Chinese Buddhism. The emphasis of Chan was meditation and seeing into one's personal nature. Within the Chan school, several different sects were founded and two sects survived. The teachings of these two sects of Chan traveled to Japan about seven centuries ago and in the Japanese language were called Zen.

OPTIONAL EXERCISES

1. Journal Entry

Write in your journal an example in your own life to demonstrate the Taoist concept of opposites in unity producing harmony.

2. Traffic Jamboree

If you become impatient driving in a traffic jam, you can change your emotional reaction to the situation by changing your thinking. You can think about something else or concentrate on listening to your radio or tape deck. You can think about the traffic congestion in a Taoist way, seeing a congested freeway as natural as a crowded animal migration route and participating by harmonizing with the traffic pattern. Instead of thinking of yourself as having been singled out for some unpleasant experience, you can see yourself and all the other drivers as involved in one of nature's patterns. You can sing, recite poetry or perform some other action to change your consciousness so that you are not victimized by unproductive, low-consciousness thoughts of conflict.

3. Harmony Exercise

Find a quiet, relaxed place to sit where you can see an expanse of water. Consider water as a symbol of the Tao, a moving force that is passive and unstoppable. Relax, look at the water and imagine yourself existing in the same harmony as the water.

4. Relativity Exercise

Prepare three bowls of water: one heated, one chilled, one near room temperature. Put your left hand in the heated water and your right hand in the chilled water. Let your hands stay in the water long enough to become accustomed to the temperatures. Next move both hands into the bowl of room temperature water. Your experience is a demonstration of the Taoist concept that all experience is relative. To understand the relative nature of any person's personal reality, imagine that the each of the two hands belonged to another person and both people told you separately about their impression of heat or cold in the last bowl.

5. Symbolic Exercise

Make a yin-yang symbol to look at. Spend whatever amount of time making it that you find pleasurable. Sit in quiet contemplation before it for a while. Taoists recommend this as the best way to access the ways of the world, better than any writings or philosophies.

CHAPTER 4

Japanese Branches

The two sects of Chan Buddhism introduced into Japan about 1700 years after Buddha's death became the Japanese Zen sects known as the Rinzai and the Soto schools. Both sects practice sitting meditation. Their major difference is that the Rinzai school places a great emphasis on the use of the Zen questions known as koans in Japanese.

The Soto Zen student sits in meditation to still individual thoughts and obtain clarity of mind for spiritual development. The Rinzai student sits in meditation to understand his Zen question for spiritual development and clarity of mind.

The original meaning of koan was official document. As used in Zen, a koan is a enigmatic expression of Zen in an anecdote or riddle. The Zen Master relates the koan to the student and the student strives to find a meaning in the anecdote or an answer to the riddle that will satisfy the master that the student is making progress.

To the student, answering the koan is like finding a meaningful image in an inkblot; the task is difficult because the meaning must satisfy the student and the Zen Master. There is no logic involved. The student conceives an answer, presents it to the Zen Master who rejects it as not showing insight, awakening, or illumination. The student returns to chores and meditation with renewed intent to find an answer acceptable to the Zen Master. This process repeats until the student finds an answer deemed satisfactory by the Zen Master. There is no one correct answer for everyone. What is sought is an answer that communicates Zen understanding to the Zen Master.

After giving a satisfactory answer to the first koan, the student is given a second koan to answer. This process is repeated until the Zen Master believes that the student is capable of answering any koan given to him.

The important aspect of the koan method is not the answer but the experience of finding an acceptable answer. This is the realization of Zen experience by the student. In order to satisfy the Zen Master, the student must find a Zen identity in the sense of understanding a natural self and the meaning of personal experience. The student cannot liberate the self until the self is perceived as something different from the self-conscious self-image known as the ego.

The koan method puts intense pressure on the student and fills the student's mind with great doubt about almost everything. This is not a unique method of teaching. Some Tantric Buddhist schools teach with riddles and enigmatic expressions. The replacement of belief with doubt is a common device among gurus and is the usual precursor to initiation in various societies or organizations. The difference in the Zen koan method is that the student must find a personal path leading out of doubt instead of receiving information from the guru, teacher, or master to replace the doubt with new beliefs. Instead of accepting dogma as truth, the student finds a personal truth acceptable to both the student and the Zen Master.

The koan is like a stone dropped into a pool, creating endless ripples as far as the eye can see. When the koan enters the mind, the ripples are small shock waves extending as far as the mind extends. These shock waves are intended to flush out the clogged mental passages, clear the channels and awaken a higher level of consciousness.

When a koan functions in this manner in a student's mind, the limitations of logic become frustratingly clear.

The amount of self-knowledge possessed by the student is perceived as inadequate. The student doesn't see anything different until he or she learns to see differently.

The Original Face Koan

One Zen Master said to a student, "Show me your original face, the face you had before your parents were born."

The student had heard that koan before but he did not know the answer. He knew that identity was not a matter of assigned names and numbers, but how could he find an identity to represent his original face?

In meditation he concentrated on the koan when he was not distracted by other thoughts but no answer came. He looked in a book with koan answers in it, but he found no answer that made sense to him.

Each time he had an appointment with the Zen Master, he gave no answer to the koan. He kept asking himself questions like: Who is this Zen Master that I should answer his questions? Why am I suffering while following the eightfold path for ending suffering? What does original face mean anyway?

When he saw the Zen Master again, the Zen Master said, "Show me your original face." The student responded, "Why should I show you my original face when it is the same as yours?"

The Rinzai student who has been given a koan by a Zen Master concentrates on that koan during meditation. The Soto student concentrates on just sitting. The purpose of the meditation is to enable the student to develop a greater awareness, a higher level of consciousness, a focus of mind that has only one point.

Zen meditation as practiced in Zen monasteries, temples, schools, and centers is a matter of intense and continuing discipline. All external aspects of meditation are ritualized. Formal Zen group meditation can be divided into five activities used in various combinations that are very similar for both Zen sects although there may be many individual differences in any particular training center:

1. Sitting
2. Walking
3. Drinking tea
4. Chanting Buddhist scripture
5. Bowing

The student sits on a small cushion or mat near a wall in the meditation hall with crossed legs so that both knees touch the floor or supporting platform. The student sits with the back straight at all times. Sitting meditation continues until the presiding official halts it. The meditator may have been instructed to pay attention to the breath, count each breath using the numbers from one to then; each time ten is reached, the meditator counts the next breath as one and continues until meditation time is over.

When the official rings a gong, a sitting period ends and a walking period begins. The students walk in a circle following the official and keeping time in time with his steps. Only the official looks where he is going; the others keep their eyes downcast and continue their concentration.

The tea ceremony was introduced to Japan along with Zen and was adopted and adapted for lay use about 500 years ago. There are various styles of tea ceremonies including those whose austerity requires only a bowl, tea, and hot water. The purpose of the tea in Zen study is to keep meditators awake; the purpose of the tea ceremony among lay people is to have a tranquil respite from the busyness of the world.

Although there is little emphasis on scripture in Zen, there is some chanting of scriptures in many training centers. This chanting requires memorization even though the scripture may be in the Chinese language as it was when introduced into Japan.

Bowing is one of the things learned in order to conform to the many rules concerning proper behavior for the Zen aspirant. The dedicated student must learn when to bow, how to bow, to whom or to what, and how many times. In those schools where meditators are struck with a stick to keep them awake, the striking ceremony may require bowing from both the striker and the struck.

Learning Experiences

Two school friends finished their schooling; one went into the military and the other went to a Zen center. Some time later they met and discussed their experiences.

The former soldier said, "I didn't like the food, the discipline and the endless rules which were randomly and selectively enforced. Most of the people in training were there not because they wanted to be but because of external pressures. All of the tasks assigned to me were menial. I spent a lot of time waiting and I never had enough time to sleep. The pay was miserably low. How was your Zen training?"

"Much the same, but I had to pay for it."

The ex-military friend said, "I learned a lot about myself in the process, but mostly I'm glad that I'll never have to be in the military again."

The Zen-trained friend said, "I learned a lot about myself, a great deal about reality, and my Zen will be with me for all of my life, whatever I do."

Zen training is oriented to producing enlightenment by consciousness raising, not to producing Zen Masters. There are very few Zen Masters in the world. Those few have the difficult task of making Zen practical and effective for a variety of students who require a variety of instructions and approaches. Zen Masters have been known to recommend an ordinary life as meditation leading to Zen understanding. Some students become nuns or monks. Some become priests. Most return to lay life.

In Japan, many Zen students are in training because their parents have sent them for the discipline, the way a student in the West might be sent to a military or other strict school. Zen Buddhism is a minority religion in Japan but Zen has had an influence on Japanese arts, crafts and daily living.

OPTIONAL EXERCISES

1. Journal Entry

Reread what you wrote in your journal about the Zen question you selected from Chapter 1 as your question. Write what you think about it now. If you feel through with that koan or if you never got engaged with the process of finding an answer, select another koan from Chapter 1 and enter it in your journal with any appropriate commentary.

2. Optional Additional Reading

If the small amount of information on Zen as practiced in Japan given in this chapter seems less than you desired, locate and read some Westerner's account of his or her personal experience studying Zen in Japan. One such book is "The Empty Mirror: Experiences in a Japanese Zen Monastery" by Janwillem van de Wetering, copyright 1973, published in hardcover by Houghton Mifflin Company and in paperback by Pocket Books.

3. Fun Exercise

Make a list of things to do that are fun for you. Do one or more of them as appropriate every time you find yourself taking either Zen or your self-image so seriously that it interferes with enjoying living.

4. Work Meditation

Make your ordinary work a form of meditation by concentrating on it. Just put your attention on it and do it the best you can without creating tension in yourself.

5. Breathing Meditation

Set aside 30 minutes of your time for breathing meditation. Wear nonrestricting clothes. Sit comfortably erect. Count your breaths up to ten and then start over with one. Pay attention to your breathing, to the place where in is replaced by out, to the space between breaths. If you forget the count, just start over with one. If other thoughts enter your mind, don't focus on them but let them leave. Keep your attention on your breathing.

If you find this exercise beneficial, continue it once or twice a day as feasible. If it causes you discomfort, it is not the exercise for you at this time.

CHAPTER 5

American Leaves

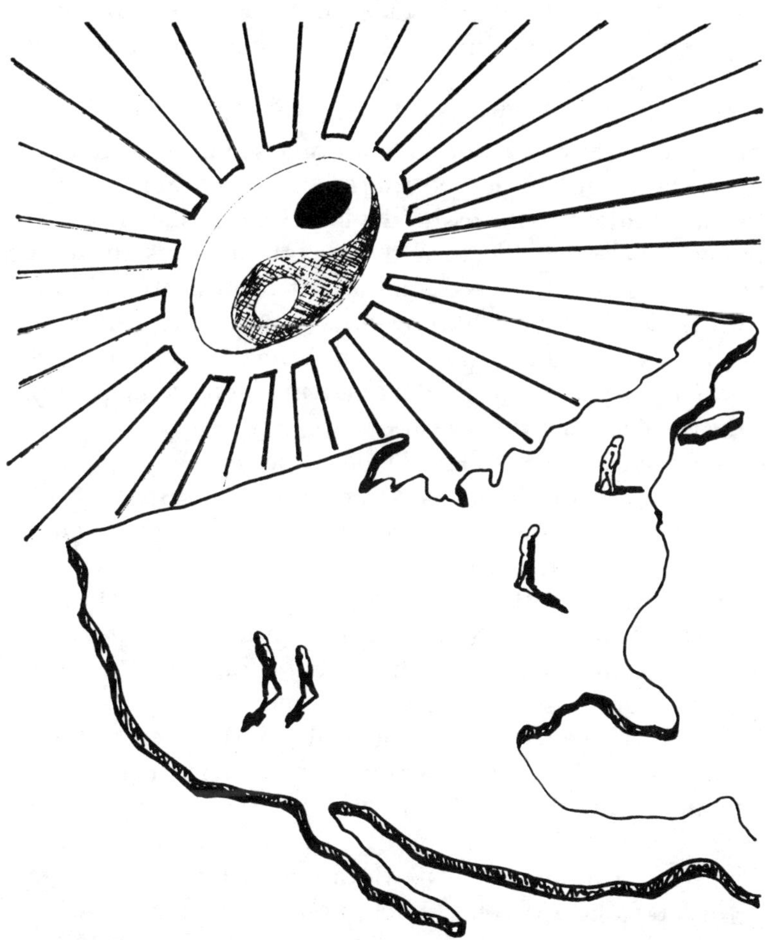

Zen Buddhism was introduced to the United States of America in 1893 by a Japanese Zen Master named Soen Shaku at the World Parliament of Religions in Chicago.

Then, as now, some Americans were interested in a religion whose aim was a great awakening; a religion with no deity to be worshipped, no creed to be accepted on faith, no dogma to be recognized as having final authority over the individual.

In 1905, Americans who had met Soen Shaku in Chicago invited him to come to San Francisco to provide Zen instruction. He was joined there by Nyogen Senzaki, his former student, who assisted him. Senzaki had left the monastery before his formal Zen training was finished because he rejected becoming a part of institutional Zen with its bureaucracy, authority, and mundane emphasis on titles, certificates, and position. When Shaku returned to Japan, Senzaki stayed. Shaku advised Senzaki not to try to teach Zen for twenty years.

Although Nyogen Senzaki had rejected the Japanese Zen hierarchy of official ranks and titles, he respected his teacher and followed his advice. He spent the next twenty years working in menial occupations, learning English, and studying Western philosophy. In 1925, he began teaching Zen in San Francisco in private residences. In 1928 he rented an apartment in San Francisco that was the first Zen Center in the United States.

Senzaki moved to Los Angeles within several years where he taught Zen and began writing about Zen. His writings began to appear in print in the 1930's. During World War II he was incarcerated at Heart Mountain Relocation Camp in Wyoming for the duration. After the war, he returned to Los Angeles. There he resumed his Zen writing and teaching. He accepted interested students without membership requirements or any organizational structure. He taught until his death in 1958.

The writings in English of a Japanese scholar named Daisetz Teitaro Suzuki (1870-1966) began to be published in the Western World in the late 1920's. His "Essays in Zen Buddhism" in three volumes (1927-1933) were many Westerners' introduction to Zen. He lectured at Tokyo University and taught in major universities in both Europe and the United States. Although a master of Zen in only the lay sense, his writings are still a major influence on Western concepts of Zen.

Although Suzuki wrote in English, many readers found his writings enigmatic and digressing at best and obscure or opaque at worst. One of the people who studied Suzuki's writings was Alan W. Watts (1915-1973). When Watts was twenty, his book, "The Spirit of Zen," was published. This book was a clarification and popularization of Suzuki's writings on Zen.

Alan Watts earned a master's degree in theology and a doctorate of divinity. He never represented himself as a Zen Buddhist but he became known as the Western world's leading interpreter of Zen in English. His "The Way of Zen," published in 1957, made Zen seem accessible to anyone who read English.

This accessibility gave Westerners an opportunity to develop a Zen orientation that was independent of the Japanese Zen hierarchy. As the interest in Zen grew, so did the number of books about Zen. Interested people could be students instead of disciples and select their own texts. They could make their own decisions as to which authors had something to teach them.

Zen in the West for many became an independent Zen that had teachers but no Zen Masters. Many Westerners who study Zen see titles and certificates as illusions of Zen, once removed from the reality of Zen when issued to an individual, twice removed from the reality of Zen in the thought of any other person.

Although there are Zen Centers that operate in the

Japanese manner in various locations in the West, many students of Zen prefer to follow a personal path of independent study and meditation. Acquiring Zen experience in a Zen Center can be rewarding for those who respond positively to the intense discipline and the numerous formal rules. However, for those students who are seeking liberation from pain, suffering, frustration, and existing belief systems, joining a group by taking a position at the bottom of a hierarchy seems at best a paradoxical approach. The following Zen story illustrates that point:

Learning from the Master

Arnold went to a Zen Center to find wisdom. He was a good student who did everything he was told. He continued meditation even when he found the required position became painful. He did the most menial work without complaint. He followed the many formal rules although he found little to value in them.

One day he packed his few belongings and prepared to leave. A monk asked Arnold, "Why are you leaving?"

Arnold replied, "I've gained the wisdom I came for."

The monk asked, "Will you tell it to me?"

Arnold said, "I've learned several things: Just as a chain is no stronger than its weakest link, a group has no higher consciousness than that of its lowest-consciousness member. I've learned that getting accustomed to pain and suffering doesn't liberate a person from it. I've learned that the Center's rules are for the benefit of the rulemakers and not the students. I've learned that the way for me to practice Zen is to pay attention to my own life; I can do that anywhere, so I am leaving."

The monk asked, "May I go with you and learn Zen from you?"

For many Westerners, the concept of master and disciple appears flawed. Many things can be learned from a teacher but to accept the teacher as spiritual master can be seen as another chain that must be broken in order to achieve spiritual liberation. If an individual accepts a spiritual master as such, then the possibility of liberation is limited by the human limitations of the master as well as of the individual. The master-disciple concept often conflicts with the Western appreciation of autonomy.

Many Westerners are also wary of joining any spiritual group that becomes a perpetuating organization. The group energy focuses on maintaining itself to the detriment of spiritual goals and the members' spiritual needs.

Because Zen is the unconventional approach to Buddhism, Zen often intrigues people interested in the unconventional. A few of these people follow Zen's conventional path at a Zen Center and learn Zen in the way things are conventionally taught to the young—with rigid discipline and a stick. Many Zen-interested people learn their Zen through the writings of Suzuki, Watts, and others who perceive meditation as much less important than one's attitude toward living, an attitude that will probably improve with a knowledge of Zen.

Some individuals are attracted to Zen because they think Zen is opposed to convention. Zen is neither opposed to or in favor of convention. Zen recognizes convention for what it is: a common way of doing things. The Zen understanding of convention is illustrated by the following story:

A Tale of Two Sailors

Vaughn, as part of his youthful rebellion, opposed convention as a self-conditioned reflex. Because he came from an army family with roots in the American Midwest, he responded to parental pressure to join the army by running away to sea. He got along well aboard ship but tended to get into trouble in most ports by behavior not in keeping with local standards.

Bert, another sailor, told Vaughn that the Captain had decided to sail without Vaughn the next time Vaughn was detained by local authorities. Vaughn said, "Damn it. You've studied Zen, Bert. You understand. Convention is stupid. I've got to fight it. How else can I wake those people up to how damn stupid it all is."

Bert said, "Convention isn't stupid. It's like a current. Use it if that's the way you want to go; otherwise leave it alone and get the wind in your sails that'll take you someplace else."

Vaughn asked, "Do you think I can learn that?"

Bert said, "Sure, Just pay attention to what you're doing. You show a lot of promise. Your first time out to sea you learned not to piss into the wind."

A sense of Zen is the inner freedom that comes from being neither in revolt against society not caught in attempts at self-justification. Through experience comes knowledge of the self that is an asset, knowledge that the self is not that social fiction called the ego. The ego holds up a false image like that seen in a distorting mirror.

The self is trusted with regulating heartbeat, breathing, metabolism and other actions that are seldom under the ego's control. Just as most people learn to have trust in these functions of the self, the rest of the self must be discovered and trusted. There is much of the self that the ego does not reflect and must be discovered through the Zen of paying attention to experience. The sense of Zen gives a trust of the self that gives life a different flavor. The modern Zen question asks: If you mistrust yourself, shouldn't you mistrust that mistrust?

Zen is correctly seen in the West not as a belief system but as a way of liberation from belief systems. Many Westerners look to Zen for self-liberation. Zen points directly at the self so the self can be discovered because it must be recognized for liberation.

The self-taught Zen that occurs in the West is a further step along the unconventional path of Zen. The convention of the Zen Master has been recognized as a convention. The Western Zen student knows that the teacher cannot teach the student who he or she is.

OPTIONAL EXERCISES

1. Journal Entry

Write in your journal: Today's date is _/_/_. Today's date is the important date from a Zen point of view.

2. Increasing Happiness Exercise

Develop the habit of telling interested people about the happy things that happen to you. Pay attention to what happens to you and others as you continue to carry out this exercise.

3. Convention Exercise

The next time you find yourself opposing convention, ask yourself the following questions. Write the answers in your journal if you think they are important.

A. What am I opposing?
B. Why am I opposing it?
C. What happens if I don't oppose it?
D. Who am I doing this for?

E. What am I learning about myself from this experience?

4. Self-discovery Exercise

Make a list in your journal of the things that your self does for you that are not normally under your conscious control

5. Ego Exercise

Write the following heading in your journal: THINGS MY EGO HAS DONE FOR ME. Leave all the space under the heading blank.

CHAPTER 6

Hip and Beat Zen Blossoms

In the 1940s and 1950s, there was an interest in Zen among some members of two groups of unconventional people, the hipsters and the beats. These people were seeking a way of life more meaningful than what was available to them in the main currents of the culture. Although some historical characters of that time are considered both hip and beat, there were differences in basic approaches to an unconventional, but satisfying life.

The hipsters were city people who saw themselves as unusually alert and knowledgeable about the human condition. They were equally aware of convention and nonconvention, able to use either to survive the changes inherent in the hip lifestyle. The ideal for the hipster was to retain that aware composure known as cool regardless of circumstances or events. Cool was not cold or withdrawn but a matter of poise, of grace under pressure. Those who were interested in Zen perceived the unruffled calm of someone who has mastered Zen as a very hip style.

Lenny Bruce was one of the comedians who included the hip viewpoint in his routines. He presented hip reality to his audience when he criticized the civil rights movement as ballyhooing middle class lifestyles for blacks and said, (paraphrased from memory) "You and I know there's got to be something better than that." Defining what that something was became a Zen koan for many hipsters.

The hip Zen understanding of koans is illustrated by the following exchange:

Otis the Elevated and Saint Gar

Otis was explaining to St. Gar how a Zen Master uses koans in Zen training. He said, "The Zen Master hangs you up by giving you a weird riddle and demanding that you explain it. As soon as you get hip enough to explain it, he lays another one on you."

St. Gar asked, "How long does the scene last?"

Otis answered, "Until you get so hip that the Zen Master can't hang you up."

St. Gar asked, "How do you know if the Zen Master is hip enough to make you hipper?"

Otis said, "That's the real hang up. If he's that hip, he might not be into teaching."

The emphasis of Zen in the hipster life was finding a practical way to apply it to the reality of a culture in which the square style was everywhere.

Very few hipsters had experience with formal Zen. Those who were interested found it either by chance from others who knew of it or by design in self study. The emphasis of Zen in the hipster life was finding a practical way to apply it to the reality of a culture in which the square style was everywhere. The hipsters were never a movement opposed to the square culture. Hipsters were individuals seeking a path in life where each could survive without undergoing pressure to conform.

The yin and yang of the hipster world was hip and square. Although squares seemed in the ascendancy, the hipster saw that both were needed to form the Taoist patterns of harmony. As disc jockey Trinidad John said, "Squares are not the enemy. Someone has to make the elevator music. Dig what's happening to you right now. You are listening to what's new in jazz, five to ten years before it's rearranged into elevator music."

Hipsters were usually night people whose slang was a verbal shorthand understood mainly by others who were hip. Many of the terms were jazz musicians' slang because nearly all hipsters loved jazz. One Zen-oriented hipster said, "The jazz club is like my meditation hall and the jazz is the subject of my meditation. Jazz has taught me that life is as it is supposed to be, a mixed bag. If you ask what jazz is, I'll say that if you don't hear it, my words can't reveal it."

The following hip Zen story illustrates how one hipster used her knowledge of Zen in her every-night life:

The Zen of Public Relations

Hazel the Hipster ran an unlicensed after-hours private club that catered to musicians, bartenders, waitresses, and

> other people who worked nights. Trinidad John was accepted for membership when a musician friend introduced him to Hazel. In a conversation some months later, John asked her what criteria she used to grant membership. She said, "Anyone who is hip enough to find this place is hip enough to be here." John said, "You've got a real mixed bag of people here—all races, all sexes—and at least a third of them want to ball you. How do you keep things cool?" Hazel said, "I use the Zen of public relations—Treat every customer the same."

The hipster took satisfaction in leading the hip life style, being alert to every nuance and every trend without becoming commonplace enough to be considered trendy. The intellectual hipsters saw the mainstream culture as full of the illusion of knowledge, which they considered the most frustrating kind of ignorance. The Zen hipster realized that thought created personal reality and used a knowledge of Zen to avoid getting hung up about it.

The beats were part of a group movement, people who distance themselves from the mainstream culture to gain a different perspective. From this perspective they developed their individual and group ideals, art, dress, behavior, and style. They sought self-expression, spontaneity and creativity. Their interest in the unconventional often included an interest in Zen.

Many beats used Zen as license. Discovering that Zen frees the self from conceptual prisons, they often abandoned concepts in art and behavior just because the concept was there. Their poetry and prose helped attract enough people that the movement became known as the Beat Generation.

Jack Kerouac's undisciplined prose gave readers Kerouac's understanding of Gary Snyder's Zen in "Dharma Bums," a lightly fictionalized account of mid 1950s California adventures; the hero, Japhy Ryder, is Snyder as seen by Kerouac. In Kerouac's "Desolation Angels," the character Jarry Wagner is Gary Snyder.

Gary Snyder is a poet and essayist who studied Zen in Japan. In 1957, Evergreen Review published his "Letter from Kyoto," telling about his experiences and beliefs. Although he saw Zen organizations as too caught up in the mainstream culture to be of much attraction to his generation, he was for many beats an introduction to Zen.

The beats applied the spontaneity of Zen as an antidote to the stuffiness of convention. They embraced change in music, poetry, and prose in an uncritical manner which Midnight Max described in a poem recited over the sound of bongo drums as "Let the one who is without Zen cast the first stone."

The beat movement attracted the attention of major magazines like "Time" and "Life." Although most articles in the major media treated the beats as somewhat amusing curiosities worthy only of mention in passing, the 1950's became the Beat Decade. Many different people in the arts were soon considered part of the Beat Generation regardless of whether they considered themselves beats or not.

Like the hipsters, the beats tended to have gathering places in cities. The American mythical city centers for the beats were Greenwich Village in New York, North Beach in San Francisco, and Venice in Los Angeles. Some beats, like the ones in the following Zen story, visited the beat areas as a religious person might visit a shrine:

North Beach, December 1957

Rudy and Jover went to San Francisco to visit a few legendary beat establishments. The major reason for the trip was to change Rudy's frame of mind; he felt low because the woman in his life had gone back East for the holidays.

They visited the City Lights bookstore, had espresso and bagels at the Co-existence Bagel Shop, and went to The Place where Red the bartender served them red wine while Edgar Allan Poet recited:

The Zen When

It's Zen
Just when
The same old grind
Is left behind
And you see all
With Buddhamind.

It's Zen
Just when
Over the rapping
And the tapping,
You hear the sound,
One hand clapping.

Rudy and Jover ate Chinese food in Chinatown. Rudy said he felt rejuvenated. Then he opened his fortune cookie and discovered a blank fortune slip inside. He asked Jover, "Does this mean my life is over?"

Jover answered, "No, It's a Zen fortune. Your life is like a white canvas ready for paint or white paper ready for words. The message is your life is your opportunity for self-expression."

The decade of the Beat Generation was the 50s. Once that decade, which the beats saw as a period of mass, unthinking conformity, ended, many of the beats began changing. In the 60s, some memorable parties were held to mark the changes—like the following one held in the Echo Park section of Los Angeles.

Rex's Goodbye Party

Rex's Goodbye to Los Angeles party featured a large sign just inside the front door. The sign read WELCOME CREAM OF THE SCUM! Everybody talked about their art, their lovers, their friends, and their changes. Only a few spoke of Zen.

When Van posed the beat Zen Koan, "Am I bound by my belief that there are boundaries?" Buddy Darma answered with a Zen Haiku poem: "Nirvana seeker, desiring to lose desire is your paradox."

OPTIONAL EXERCISES

1. Journal Entry

Without advance thought, spontaneously write in your journal your reactions to the chapter just read.

2. Spontaneous Walking Exercise

Take a walk without planning where you are going. At each corner take the most interesting direction.

3. Listening Exercise

Find an opportunity to listen to what was called progressive jazz in the 50s. Listen to what critics considered the best of 50s jazz and write your response to it in your journal. If you have a positive response to this music, use it for meditation. Just sit quietly in comfortable clothes and concentrate on the sounds. Write about your experience in your journal.

4. Writing Exercise

Write a poem of any length about Zen. Enter the poem in your journal.

5. Shrine Exercise

Select a particular place from your memory that could serve as a personal shrine. Visit it in person or in memory. Write about your experience in your journal.

CHAPTER 7

Counter Culture Zen Flowers

During the 1960's there were enough people searching for alternatives to various aspects of convention that a counter culture movement was apparent. The counter culture looked for answers to questions previously considered too painful to be asked or too profound to be answered. The decade was one of liberation; some counter culture people sought liberation through Zen.

Jazz lost its position as the music of the nonconformists. The music of the 60's was rock and roll; the majority of the young had grown up with it and were able to enjoy it with or without knowledge about it. Often the lyrics seemed to say little more than "Love the kinks in your brain; dance with them in the rain." Some lyrics seemed to be asking a Zen question—Does freedom mean nothing left to lose?

A variety of people were involved in counter culture activities. While there was general agreement that change was needed, there was a great deal of disagreement about what changes should be implemented and in what manner. The 60s were marked by excesses in politics, sex, religion, and various other activities by groups and individuals. Many visionaries saw a cultural renaissance as imminent; others foresaw a revolution, as in this 60s Zen story:

The Zen Revolution

Bert, after giving a lecture on Zen, answered questions from the audience. The first question was: "What relationship does Zen have with revolution?"

Bert replied, "In Zen, the revolution takes place inside you when you become one with your experience. As your experience changes, so do you. When you realize that your efforts toward changing the world make more changes in you than in the world, then the Zen revolution is complete."

The counter culture was divided on the subject of revolution. Some thought that the changes required to make the world a better place for everyone demanded revolution. Others preached evolution. One Zen lecturer said, "Be accepting of change as part of the spontaneity of reality."

The war in Vietnam was a major force in the lives of many Americans in the 60s. The popular culture said the war was a political necessity: the counter culture said that American involvement in the war was a tragic mistake.

The extreme right said the American draftees were patriots: the extreme left said that the American draftees were prisoners of war. Those with an opinion that differed from these extremes were often criticized by extremists on both ends of the spectrum. As Felix the Philosopher said then, "The difference between a patriot and a mass murderer is often no more than politics." Zenedict Arnold said, "Keeping a consistent political position will eventually make you guilty of treason."

One student of martial arts and Zen got classified as a conscientious objector when he told the draft board that he would defend himself from physical assault but he wouldn't kill someone for having bad politics just as he wouldn't kill someone for having bad taste.

The term hippie, which had previously meant an unsophisticated imitation of hipster, was commonly applied to many individuals in the counter culture. Among the hippies, race, religion, and background were unimportant if an individual seemed to be a compatible person. Hippies were searching for joyful alternatives to what they considered low-consciousness practices in the mainstream culture.

In the 60s sexually transmitted diseases were considered easily curable by most people. Better methods of birth control made unwanted pregnancies more avoidable. The belief that sex could be enjoyed without physical complications created a new era of recreational sex.

Some of the hippies found the practice of sexual freedom a source of liberation. Some groups were strong in practice; others were strong in idealism. One sexually oriented group alluded to the sexual idealism in one science fiction novel by including this haiku in their introductory material:

Thirsting by the water,
A stranger in a strange land,
You are no tourist.

The sexually free hippies often lived in communes. Initially many of these communes were city oriented. Some later moved to rural areas like the one mentioned in this story:

The Zen of Cooking

Gordon grew up in the kitchen of his family's restaurant. In the 60s he opened his own small country cafe where he practiced Zen by paying complete attention to whatever task was at hand.

Occasionally, one or more of the members of a sexually free commune ate in Gordon's cafe. Gordon had heard that they sometimes invited outsiders to an orgy. He cultivated one of the women from the commune who was interested in Gordon's Zen of cooking. Eventually, she invited him to the commune for a feast.

Gordon, hoping that feast was just another name for sex orgy, accepted the invitation. At the commune, he was disappointed to see that many of the visitors were local couples with children. Gordon knew then that there would be no orgy so he concentrated on the food. When he thanked his hostess, she asked him if the food had disappointed him. Gordon said the food was good but that he had secretly hoped the feast would be an orgy. His hostess said, "You always talked to me about food. I thought that was what you were interested in. Come back tomorrow and I'll teach you the Zen of accepting responsibility for what you want and asking for it."

Zelda, one of the Zen-oriented people interested in sexual expression in sexual freedom, said of the 60s sexual attitudes and habits. "Never have so many people been so aware that sex is far too important to take seriously."

The following sexual liberation story captures some of the sexual openness that was prevalent in the 60s:

Julian's California Adventure

Julian came west to San Francisco in his search for liberation. In a sexual fantasy workshop, Julian expressed his fascination with the idea of having sex with a horse. One woman said that she owned a female horse that Julian was welcome to meet and if it was okay with her horse then it was okay with her. Julian went to meet the horse the next day. When he returned, one of his friends asked him about the experience.

Julian said, "I grew up in an eastern city, watching cowboy shows and admiring horses. Today I had an opportunity to get near a horse for the first time. I was so sexually tuned on that I thought I was ready for anything. But nothing had prepared me for the way horses smell. That turned me off completely."

His friend said, "I'm sorry it turned into a bummer."

Julian said, "It really changed my life, but I learned a lot from it. Now I'm going to liberate myself from excessive idealism."

Sex was often central to the life of hippies who were sexually free. As Kokomo Dragonlady said, "If you think sex is just for making babies, you aren't ready for parenthood." The happy hippie who called himself Huckleberry Zen expressed his beliefs about life with a sexual simile: "Life is like a sexual act—if you can't wait for the end or if you want it to go on forever, you don't understand it."

In the 60s there were more people coming into maturity than ever before. But not all the people in the counter culture were under 30. Otis, who was older than the Beatles, said these words about aging in a Zen lecture:

Otis on Aging

If you worship being young, you'll spend your middle years mourning your lost youth and your later years mourning your wasted middle years. Being young has its kicks

> and its bruises; every age has its ups and downs. People who put down others on the basis of age, whether younger or older, are immature. Many people think they'll die young because their ego has told them so. The ego lies! That's the same ego that tells them they are indestructible and will live forever. We all know that the death rate is 100 percent. The Zen of living is aging one day at a time gracefully. That's the manifestation of grace under pressure.

The counter culture contributed to many changes in the 60s. Some counter culture ideas and actions faded from view; others have become part of the popular culture. The Zen of the counter culture often had a timeless quality as in these words of Huckleberry Zen:

"If you want control, get control over yourself. When you are free of the desire to control others, you have found control."

"Everything that has happened has got you where you are. If you can't see where you're going, make sure you're not focused on where you've been."

"A competent spiritual teacher will give you insights and common sense; an incompetent teacher will give you common prejudice and nonsense. Alert students learn to tell the difference."

"How other see you is the shadow of the self."

"Zen turns the crap in your life to fertilizer."

"Anyone who says, 'I've got all the answers,' doesn't pay attention to questions."

OPTIONAL EXERCISES

1. Journal Entry

Write in your journal what is most memorable in the chapter just read and why you remember it.

2. Experience Expansion

Expand your awareness of what aging is by paying attention to your encounters with people outside your general age group.

3. Prospective Parenting Exercise

If you are not yet a parent but may become one, spend enough time with babies and young children as well as their parents to get familiar with parenting and your reactions to the process. If you are a parent already, just keep paying attention to what you are doing.

4. Conventional Checking Exercise

Make a list of your actions that don't conform to conventional standards. Examine the personal reality that prompts such actions with the knowledge that you can change your thoughts. Your thoughts can change your feelings and changed thoughts or feelings can change behavior.

5. Unconventional Checking Exercise

Make a list of your actions that conform to conventional standards. If any of these actions are undesirable to you, examine what possible alternatives exist and what the consequences would be. Be aware that the price paid for nonconformity in many areas is often within reason.

CHAPTER 8

Discordian Zen Bouquets

The Discordian Society was formed in the 1950s by Kerry Thornley and Gregory Hill as a vehicle for satiric art, amusement, and entertainment. Discordians recognize the divinity of Eris, the Goddess of Discord, Chaos, Confusion, and Bureaucracy who was known to the ancient Greeks as Eris but known to the ancient Romans as Discordia. The Discordian Society is a nonprofit, multi-prophet religion with no fees, no dues, no organization, no membership roster, and no membership requirements. According to Hill, "One becomes a member of the Discordian Society by (a) presuming the existence of such a society and by (b) defining this society such that it includes oneself."

Both founders were interested in Zen. The Discordian Society Bible is "Principia Discordia," the magnum opiate of Malaclypse the Younger (alias Gregory Hill). Although mostly written by Hill, this book also contains Zen koans and Zen stories written by Thornley, Robert Anton Wilson, and other, almost all credited to Discordian aliases. One Discordian koan asks, "If Eris isn't in charge, where did all the chaos come from?"

Just as Japanese Zen has two schools, the Soto and the Rinzai, Discordian Zen has two schools, DeSoto and DeRenzy. Both schools were created by the Zen Discordian who uses the alias Buddy Darma. His satirical instructions require the DeSoto disciple to meditate in a sitting position similar to that of a person sitting in the back seat of an old DeSoto four-door automobile and wait for illumination to come like a car dome light coming on. The DeRenzy disciple is required to sit and watch the sexually explicit films directed by Alex DeRenzy and seek illumination in the film's lighting effects.

Desoto

When asked about the DeSoto instructions, Buddy Darma replied, "DeSoto disciples are instructed to sit in the back seat to prevent them from driving away from illumination in case they materialize the entire car. There were a few problems with disciples who did that. They weren't prepared for the traffic."

Buddy Darma states that the DeRenzy disciples are to "watch the films with awareness and without popcorn. Keep watching until insight is achieved. Keep the insight secret until it leads to personal behavior change. If the behavioral change doesn't get the disciple arrested for immorality or declared obscene by loco standards, then the insight is valid."

Derenzy

During the 60s, several Discordians patronized the West Los Angeles coffeehouse formerly called The Blue Couch and renamed The New Balladeer. When the new owner repainted the unisex restroom, he invited two Discordian writers with the aliases Omar and Giovanni to change the bare white walls into sources of inspiration by the addition of profound graffiti. Here are some of the Discordian wall readings that carry a Zen flavor:

"Free Play for Narcissists"

"It's your body—love it or leave it."

"All bigots are equal."

"A person who can't reason is a bigot. A person who won't reason is a fool. A person who dares not reason is a slave. a person who uses reason as his or her only tool is a prisoner in a self-made cage."

"Telling the truth works better than squelching the rumors."

"Don't expect perfection in others even if you suspect you have found it in yourself."

"Life becomes easier when you realize you can liberate yourself."

"This is Lenny Bruce Memorial Shrine Number Five. Did he die of the crap you're taking?"

"Abandon is the key to opening your head. The most difficult thing to abandon is outmoded but cherished ideas."

"Try out your weapons on yourself before using them on others."

"Unquestioning faith or unassessed skepticism cause mental constipation."

"The past is only in your thoughts. Keep the wisdom and the pleasant memories and be willing to let the rest go."

"Keep those chips off your shoulder; they spoil the drape of your clothes."

"History is more than the lies that survive cultural processes; it is a reflection cast by humanity's evolving consciousness."

"If all you know is the price, forget it."

"Growing older is the only alternative to death."

"Great oafs from little icons grow."

"May the illusions you choose not to lose bring you infinite joy."

"Once you know truth you find it everywhere—even here—and suddenly truth surrounds you, free for the taking."

"You make yourself who you are. The process is slow sculpture."

When they finished their wall writing, Omar asked, "What if people are confused by these messages?" Giovanni replied, "Before every great insight, there is a period of confusion. If we don't make people aware in any other way, we will make them aware that they are confused."

Discordians often used business-sized cards printed with Discordian slogans. Hill satirized conventional religion with cards that ordained the bearer as a Discordian Pope. Thornley alerted people to a higher consciousness reality by distributing cards that read: THERE IS NO ENEMY ANYWHERE. Dolly Lama issued, when appropriate, the consciousness-raising card that stated: "Be moderate in all things, especially moderation." Wilma, the Witch from Wichita, had cards inscribed as follows: "A spell has been cast that will bring you happiness, success, and enlightenment. Don't screw it up by acting like a shithead." Kokomo Dragonlady, the Indian from Indiana, designed cards that read "Life is a mirror effect. What you send out is what is reflected to you."

As part of their religious satire, Discordians recognize a variety of saints, some of them fictional in origin. St. Yossarian, the Patron Saint of Sanity, is the character in

Joseph Heller's war novel, "Catch 22," who, caught up in the insanity of the war, realizes that he has become insane. He reports this to the base psychiatrist and requests a psychiatric discharge. The psychiatrist tells Yossarian that he can't get a discharge because of a catch in the regulations—catch 22, which says that personnel who are sane enough to recognize that they are crazy are not crazy enough for discharge. the following Zen story is about a Discordian who understood St. Yossarian:

He reported himself as mentally unfit for duty.

Catch 22 Revisited

When Hypoc finished his medical training as a psychiatrist, he was drafted into the military. He subsequently became the base psychiatrist on an island in southeast Asia. There, his duty included deciding who should be sent back to the States for possible psychiatric discharge and who should be returned to duty. Hypoc developed his own criterion—anyone that Hypoc thought capable of convincing the stateside examining board that he was insane got a helping hand from Hypoc. When Hypoc wanted his own discharge, he reported himself as mentally unfit for duty. Since Hypoc was the authority, he was sent back to the States for observation. Hypoc got his discharge.

In the late 60s and in the early 70s, several Discordians moved from Los Angeles to northern California and settled temporarily in San Francisco and Sonoma County. Gregory Hill, using several Discordian aliases and a San Francisco post office box. began disbursing Discordian information on a wider basis mostly through the mail. Discordians everywhere were invited to send postage stamps, copies of Discordian material to be distributed, and any unneeded business reply envelopes bearing the legend, POSTAGE WILL BE PAID BY ADDRESSEE. Those envelopes were stuffed with many messages like the following Zenlike put on:

GAME RULES

1. The player must pretend to take the rules and structure of the game seriously.

2. The player must forget that he or she is only pretending.

This is your copy of the agreement you made when you elected to live in this world. Don't forget to pretend to take it seriously.

One of the Zen Discordians was stopped in San Francisco by a young convert to a cult that sold propaganda and products on the street. The convert was inadequately clothed, looked hungry, and was suffering from the cold. Instead of a sale, the cultist was told how following Buddha's path could end suffering. The cultist asked, "Will that really work?" The reply was, "Even if it doesn't, it's a better life than hustling strangers on the street."

When Omar arrived in Sonoma County, he found Giovanni working a job that was wrecking his health and asked him why he didn't quit. Giovanni said he couldn't quit and get his money out of the retirement fund unless he had a letter from a doctor saying it was necessary for his health. Omar called Hypoc who said he would sign the letter if Omar would type it. Hypoc refused payment for this favor, so Giovanni gave him a Zen blessing: May the wisdom you achieve be not only the gaining of usual knowledge but also the shedding of illusion. Hypoc asked, "Isn't most of usual knowledge illusion?" Giovanni replied, "I see the blessing is working already."

The Discordian Society is still growing despite having no center for information or recruitment. St. Robert the Orderly, when asked to explain this at a Zen lecture, said, "Of all the great, one true religions, Discordianism offers the most fun."

OPTIONAL EXERCISES

1. Journal Exercises

Write in your journal an insight from this chapter that is meaningful to you. What behavioral change in you is associated with this insight.

2. Discordian Mail Exercise

Create or assemble some material that seems Discordian to you. Stuff it into a business reply envelope that says addressee will pay postage and mail it. If you find the experience satisfying, repeat it when feasible.

3. Discordian Telephone Exercise

The next time you get a junk phone call from some low-consciousness person who invades privacy at random, tell the phone solicitor that he or she has reached the Discordian Society Sales Network and ask what he or she wants to buy. Do not hesitate to offer impossible bargains at unbelievable savings. Ask the phone solicitor for a home address and telephone number so sales personnel can advertise future sales by telephone calls, mail, and personal visits. Keep trying to sell the phone solicitor something until he or she hangs up.

4. Discordian Conversion Exercise

When approached by any religious proselytizer, explain that you know the world is controlled by the Goddess Eris who had turned their group into a bunch of public nuisances as a step on their path to the great, one true religion of Discordianism. Ask for the home address so you can send information and missionaries. Do not hesitate to make wild, exaggerated, and unsubstantiated claims. Be as inventive and aggressive as possible until the person leaves your presence. Follow them and continue your spiel if you really get into it.

5. Acceptance Exercise

If you performed one or more of these exercises and enjoyed it, accept yourself as a member of the Discordian Society who enjoys meaningful religious rituals. If you discover or invent other satisfactory rituals, share them with other people, especially Discordians.

CHAPTER 9

An Independent Zen View of Meditation

Meditation is often needlessly made mystical and mystifying by various sects, traditions, and teachers. From an independent Zen point of view, there is nothing mysterious about the process or its purpose. Most of the ritual, ceremony, rules, and requirements are superfluous embellishments to a simple act.

In Zen, meditation consists of focusing the attention on one thing to the exclusion of others.

In Zen, meditation consists of focusing the attention on one thing to the exclusion of others. This one-pointedness of mind, developed through discipline, calms the mind and leads to the raising of consciousness. In the Zen sense, meditation is not prayer, which is an attempt to link individual consciousness to an external higher consciousness, nor is it contemplation, daydreaming, or any other activity carried on by the mind in its everyday thinking mode. Meditation is a state of consciousness distinct from the three ordinary states of consciousness: sleeping, dreaming, and wakefulness. The meditative state is characterized by a metabolic rate lower than sleep and by relaxation and calmness greater than that experienced during sleep.

When Buddha recognized that the masochistic pursuit of self-denial tended to strengthen the ego instead of producing a higher state of consciousness, he abandoned asceticism and found the answers to his questions through meditation. This is the foundation for the emphasis on meditation in Zen. This emphasis is exaggerated in the mythical acts of the semi-fictional Bodhidharma, an Indian Buddhist who traveled overland to China as a missionary. Allegedly, Bodhidharma, unable to attract followers, meditated for nine years facing a wall, before finding a disciple. During that nine year period, Bodhidharma had so little acceptance of his own nature that he ripped off his eyelids in self-disgust over falling asleep while meditating.

From an independent Zen point of view, Bodhidharma, like most missionaries, had an enlarged ego problem because he believed that his personal reality was more desirable for others than their own; Bodhidharma's meditation became his own trap of self-denial, strengthening the ego with the concept of overcoming adversity through stoic effort. Fortunately, Bodhidharma was exposed to the Taoist way of observing nature and realized the unnaturalness of his actions. The traditional Zen viewpoint recognizes the value of the Taoist aspects of Zen but retains a belief in the value of unnaturally long periods of meditation.

The preparation for independent Zen meditation consists of the following steps:

1. The meditator should schedule a time and place to meditate twice a day for approximately 15 minutes each time. Ideally, the time and place should be consistently the same with no interruptions likely. The time should be when the stomach is empty. The place should be somewhere where the meditation docs not inconvenience others or focus attention on the meditator.

2. The meditator should have a clock or watch visible during meditation. An alarm should be set to end the meditation period if the meditator is concerned about falling asleep or meditating longer than the allotted time.

The procedure for individual Zen meditation is simple:

1. The meditator should sit in a comfortable position and relax the body so that indication of bodily discomfort do not interfere with meditation.

2. The meditator, with eyes closed or lowered, breathing normally, begins counting: one with the first exhalation, two with the first inhalation, three with second inhalation, and continuing until the number ten in reached. Then the mediator repeats the counting, beginning again with number one.

3. If the meditator looses count, he or she should begin again with the number one. If a thought intrudes on the

meditation, the meditator should recognize it as a passing thought. Let it pass on out, and continue counting by focusing on the breath.

4. When the allotted time is over, the meditator should take a moment or more to reorient to the non-meditative state and then go on with everyday activities.

Many people are surprised that they lack the discipline to concentrate on their breathing for 15 minutes. The discipline becomes easier with practice. Most people begin to notice positive physical and mental effects from meditation within a two-week period. Anyone who has a negative reaction to this type of meditation—a reaction other than the mind's opposition to discipline—should not continue with breathing meditation but might consider another type of meditation.

The usual benefits from meditation are an improved attitude toward personal experience and a feeling of being more relaxed, healthier, and more alert. Meditation is a highly individual experience that is not competitive or comparative. The meditative state is somewhat like the point between waking and sleeping where the mind is not aware of the body and unusual thoughts and images may flicker in the mind.

Some of the exceptional things that happen in meditation are mentioned in this Zen meditation story:

Otis's Meditation Class

The first night of meditation class, one student asked Otis, the teacher, if he considered himself a Zen Master. He said, "I am a Zenster, a Zen-oriented hipster who is independent of, and indifferent to, the established hierarchies of Zen."

Another student asked Otis if he considered himself to be enlightened. He replied, "Enlightenment is a state of consciousness like any other and individuals drift in and out of it. I consider myself more enlightened today than yesterday and less enlightened than I will be tomorrow.

After a few meetings, the first student asked if the development of psychic abilities was common in meditators and what does it mean? Otis responded, "Whenever that happens to my students, I tell them to feel free to use any new abilities they develop as long as it doesn't interfere with their meditation."

Another student told Otis that he had a vision of Buddha while meditating and he felt that in his next meditation, Buddha would speak to him. Otis said, "If he speaks, ask him what your last breath count was. That will help you get over petty distractions and get on with your meditation."

Breath counting is not the only form of meditation that creates one-pointedness of mind by the discipline of focusing on one thing only. Mantra meditation, also known as transcendental meditation, focuses the meditator's attention on mentally repeating a mantra. Any set of syllables can be an effective mantra for the interested meditator. Some sample mantras are:

Mantra

Alpha

Zenith

Nada

Tee Em

Mentally reciting a mantra, like breath counting, is an internally created focus for the mind. An external focus on sound can also be an effective focus as illustrated by this meditation story:

The Spiritual Exercise Meditation

Having heard about a powerful spiritual training organization in downtown Los Angeles, Giovanni went to one of their meetings. He was told that he would have to sit outside the exercise hall during ten spiritual exercise sessions before he could be allowed inside and initiated. After initiation he would be allowed to participate fully.

Giovanni learned from Barry, another potential initiate, that sitting outside for ten sessions was a new requirement for initiation, designed to exclude curiosity seekers and people prone to psychotic breaks during the spiritual initiations. While sitting outside during the first session, Giovanni listened to the composite sound coming from the exercise hall. Because the sound was ever changing and too complex for meaningful aural analysis, Giovanni focused on just listening and lost himself in the timelessness of meditation until the session ended.

At the next session, Giovanni again experienced the fullness of meditation. At the coffee break that followed the session, he saw Barry who had just been initiated. Barry told him that the initiation was a group high experience that was enjoyable but lacked the mystery that made the outside sitting meditation so complete.

Several weeks later, Barry told Giovanni that he was dropping out of the organization because of diminished returns. Giovanni talked to some other members initiated after sitting outside and found their experience similar. Consequently, he recorded the next session from his outside sitting position and he never came back for initiation.

He told Barry what he had done and said, "Group highs are widely available but effective meditation aids are too valuable to lose.

Regardless of how much imagination a meditator has, meditation when practiced becomes simpler than ever imagined. Initially there is the boredom of disciplining the mind. Both boredom and tiredness can lead to falling asleep during meditation. The meditator can avoid the problem of sleepiness during meditation by sleeping an adequate amount. If the meditator has trouble falling asleep at the end of a full day, the following meditation can be used to guide the meditator into restful sleep:

The Countdown Meditation to Induce Sleep or Rest

In a place appropriate for sleep the meditator should assume a position comfortable for sleeping. Starting at 99 for the first breath, the meditator should count down one number with each following breath. Any thought floating to the surface of the mind is allowed to drift away with minimum attention. If the number is lost, the meditator can start again with the last number remembered or with 99. Usually some time before zero is reached, the meditator is relaxed or asleep.

The value of meditation is widely recognized, but the experience is highly subjective. Each meditator must make the individual decision as to whether meditation is part of the spiritual path that he or she chooses to travel now or in the future.

OPTIONAL EXERCISES

1. Journal Entry

Write in your journal what your experience with meditation has been in general terms.

2. Meditation Exercises

If you are not now a meditator, try breath counting or mantra meditation. Have patience with the discipline. Unless the experience is too unpleasant to continue, meditate twice a day for 15 minutes each time for at least two weeks. Write about your experience in your journal. After two weeks, decide whether or not the benefits or potential benefits are sufficient for you to continue.

3. Countdown Meditation

The next time you are tired but sleep eludes you, try the countdown meditation. Write the results in your journal after you awaken.

4. Sound Meditation

Listen to one of your favorite instrumental musical selections as if it were intended as a meditation guide. Write your experiences in your journal.

5. Group High Experience

Write in your journal the difference you detect in the group high experience and the experience of successful meditation.

CHAPTER 10

Intuition

Intuition, defined as an immediate comprehension not based on rational or logical thought, is an important part of Zen. Koans and meditation both stimulate the development of intuition. Finding the answer to a koan frustrates the rational mind and demands an intuitive answer. Meditation creates the one-pointedness of mind that promotes intuition.

The rational mode of consciousness is analytical and sequential, concerned largely with the mental interpretation of sensory data. The intuitive mode of consciousness is receptive and holistic, concerned with knowledge that is based on perceptions largely ignored by the rational mode of consciousness. Together they are the yin and yang of consciousness. Both modes are necessary for completeness, but many cultures emphasize only the rational mode.

Human cultures deal with the world as if there were a stable, objective reality discernible to all. This cultural process produces an illusion of objective reality which is acceptable to a cultural majority. This illusion limits awareness by requiring individuals to ignore information that conflicts with the cultural model of reality. Most intuition information is ignored by the culture because the information doesn't fit neatly into the cultural model of reality.

Each culture encourages individuals to develop a rational mode of consciousness as a necessity for biological survival. The individual, through the rational consciousness, learns to provide the food, water, protection, and environment required for life to continue. In effect, this process makes the individual become a parent to the self. During the process, the individual creates a self image, commonly called the ego, to deal with cultural reality. This self image is a social fiction which does not exist unless thought about. Some individuals intuitively recognize the ego as a distorted shadow of the self. Those who do mistake the ego for the self attempt to be a parent to the ego, an unending, thankless, impossible task.

The individual, based on feedback from the culture, learns to construct a personal reality focused on survival within a particular culture. Individuals who equate their subjective personal reality to an allegedly objective reality discernible to those outside the culture are caught in a cultural trance which limits their consciousness.

Some individuals within a culture repress almost all of their intuitive abilities because they are fearful of any aspects of reality that are not culturally endorsed. Intuition in most cultures is inhibited by neglect as a part of the cultural process. Developing intuition frequently requires breaking the cultural trance and overcoming some cultural prejudice. The cultural model of reality doesn't recognize its limitations and presents cultural prejudices as objective reality. As long as an individual believes that accidents of birth—time, place, nationality, race, ethnic mixture, gender, culture—are more important than the self who experiences these accidents, that individual's consciousness is limited by the cultural trance. All or part of the trance can be broken by continuing feedback that indicates a reality greater than the cultural model or by the intuitive knowledge that cultural reality is a limitation to be surpassed.

In some individuals the cultural trance is so extensive that they perceive the fiction of the culture as fact. Some television soap opera watchers believe the actors are the characters they portray and that the drama is real life. Herb, a Zen-oriented actor who played a sympathetic figure in a daytime drama, was often addressed in public by fans as Ed, the character he portrayed. One day in a grocery store, a fan walked up to Herb and said, "Ed, I think I ought to tell you that your boss is going to fire you." Herb replied, "It's my job as an actor to act like I don't know that. Thank you for telling me I'm doing a good job."

One of the most effective ways of breaking the cultural trance is exposure to other cultures. For some individuals, entering another culture shatters many cherished ideas about reality and creates culture shock, decreasing the person's ability to function. As one Peace Corps Veteran said, "The more I traveled, the more I realized that objective reality is a subjective illusion created by individual thought. Every human being lives in a world that is different from every other person's world. I'm not saying that there isn't any reality; I'm saying that reality is different for everybody. Common reality is whatever there is that doesn't go away when you stop believing in it."

Breaking the cultural trance is an important step on the path of self discovery and liberation. Some individuals intuitively seek the experience of culture shock to end the cultural trance. As one traveler said about his trip to Japan, "I landed in Japan with everything I owned in my backpack. No one was expecting me and there wasn't anywhere I had to go. I didn't know the language or the culture. I had never felt so free in all my life."

Because the rational mode of consciousness is developed by the culture, Zen concentrates on developing the intuitive mode of consciousness to give the individual an expanded, more complete consciousness. Zen is nonintellectual in the sense that the experience of Zen is mostly intended for recognizing and developing the intuitive mode of consciousness. Zen is not anti-intellectual in any sense because the teachings of Zen stress learning from all experience including the intellectual, the intuitive, and the entire spectrum of the life as it is lived.

All individuals have intuition. A common human experience is the intuitive feeling of being stared at. Almost everyone experiences this at some time when there is no discernible way for the starer to have been seen or heard. This is innate intuitiveness saying that something is happening that may affect individual survival.

Many people have experienced hearing the telephone ring and being certain who was calling even though the call was not expected by the rational mode of consciousness. These experiences of premonitions or hunches are intuitive, creative leaps toward reality. Because the information is not based on deduction from the rational accumulation of data, the information may not be valued but dismissed as lucky guesses.

Another common intuitive experience is this: A visitor at the home of two friends realizes that he or she must have interrupted an intense argument although both friends are trying to behave normally. Usually the realization takes a few minutes. During that time, the rational mode of consciousness may not be aware of the data that conflicts with the facade being presented. Any number of clues might be gathered by the intuitive sense. Perhaps the body language doesn't match the words spoken. Possibly the rate of eye blinking is four or five times the normal rate of fifteen per minute, a certain indicator of stress. Maybe the rhythms of movement are slightly out of synchronization. The intuitive sense of having interrupted an argument comes into the mind as sudden knowledge without the rational mode of consciousness being aware of the process that produced the insight.

Although few cultures emphasize intuition, every culture provides many opportunities for using intuition. The following modern Zen story shows how one therapist used his intuition.

Sam's Intuition

Sam, a Zen-oriented therapist, held psychodramas that were open to the public. By using his knowledge of psychology and the techniques of the theater, he would select a person from the audience to star in his or her own life and help that person with the problems of human existence. Sometimes he would ask for a volunteer; most of the time he selected someone on an intuitive basis.

One evening, Sam asked John if he would come onto the stage and be the focus of the psychodrama. Sam soon established that John's problem in searching for a wife was that John was still focused on the first woman he loved. He revealed how he had cultivated her parents and charmed her friends while offering her the kind of romantic marriage that many women dream about. She accepted his proposal. John later realized that she was willing to marry him but that she didn't love him. He broke the engagement and moved to another state to start a new life that eventually brought him to the psychodrama.

Sam had one of the actresses in the audience play the part of John's lost love. Coached by Sam, her last lines to John were, "I liked you as much an any man I knew. My friends thought you were right for me. My parents wanted me to marry you. I had a lot of problems I hadn't told you about. I thought agreeing to marry you would solve them but it just created another one. You offered me what looked like the perfect marriage. I did my best to respond. You told me my best wasn't good enough."

Sam told John, "For years you've seen yourself as the victim in that romance. What about her? She was offered what everyone in her life told her she should want and she didn't get it. Stop holding on. Let go of the idea that you're a victim of your past. That's over. See things from her point of view and release your mental grip on her. It's time to stop thrashing around in yesterday's trash and live your life as it is today."

John felt suddenly free from the past that had occupied his thoughts for years. His mind seemed clear and his future seemed to hold promise. He asked Sam, "How did you happen to pick me tonight?"

Sam replied, "There was something about the way you looked or the way you moved that told me you were troubled. Intuitively, I felt that I could help."

OPTIONAL EXERCISES

1. Journal Entry

Write in your journal any intuitive experience that you've had. Any time your have a flash of intuition, remember it and write it in your journal. Don't be concerned if some of your intuitive flashes aren't useful or completely correct. Logic and rationality don't always produce useful results either. Writing about your intuition is intended to make it more real for you.

2. Experience Expansion

Allow room in your thinking for premonitions and hunches. When it seems appropriate and free of possible undesirable consequences, act on them.

3. Intuitive Visualization Exercise

Imagine that you have a receiver like a television screen in your mind. Visualize it. Imagine that intuitive signals exist just as television signals do and it is just a matter of tuning in. Whenever you need answers, imagine tuning your receiver to an intuitive channel and look for the information.

4. Dream Checking Exercise

Whenever you have a dream that you remember, write it down if you think it may contain intuitive information. Continue this procedure if it seems to strengthen your intuition.

5. Intuition Exercise

Devise a personal exercise to increase intuition. If it works, broaden its application. If it doesn't work, devise another exercise.

CHAPTER 11

The Zen of Self-Discovery

Before the self can be liberated, the self must be discovered.

Zen is a way of liberation, not for a culture but for the individual self. Before the self can be liberated, the self must be discovered. The process of self-discovery is the accumulation of self-knowledge.

Recognizing that each human being is a unique individual is frequently the prelude to understanding that each individual must find a personal answer to the identity problem. As one actor said to another in an improvisational scene, "When I ask, 'Who are you?' I'm asking, 'Where do you invest your identity?' Don't give me the information you use to answer questions on official forms. That's just statistics. Tell me what's important in your life. Tell me what you are doing in your life that is meaningful to you. Tell me what you have learned about yourself from your own experience. I want to relate to the inner you that only you can reveal."

Because of the necessary emphasis on survival in cultural teachings, the individual is taught to behave according to standards that originate outside of the self in the culture. The individual in relating to the culture and the individuals within it creates an inner self-image called the ego. Just as the cultural model of reality is often mistaken for objective reality, the ego is often mistaken for the self.

The Zen emphasis on paying attention to experience helps individuals realize that the ego is a construct of the imagination. When the physical being is hungry, the mind thinks of imaginary meals that are savored by the ego; one good meal can satisfy the body but the hunger of the ego just disappears when no longer thought about. The individual who doesn't recognize this process in its many forms, can easily become trapped in behavior that services the ego and neglects the self.

Recognizing that the ego is not the self is a giant step on the path of self-discovery. Learning that the insatiable demands of the ego are creations of the mind frees the individual to experience the personal reality of the self. Once a person ceases to use thought to validate ego-oriented concepts, the knowledge that the self exists separate and distinct from the ego frees that person for further self-discovery.

Self-discovery is a personal exploration of the inner space of personal reality. This is life's big adventure, with equal access to all. This modern Zen story tells of one person's joyful acceptance of her own reality:

Wanda's Wonder

When Wanda became dissatisfied with her life, she began a search for the happiness that she felt had always just barely eluded her. She read a number of self-help books, went to several lectures, talked to friends who seemed to be happier than she was, and tried several methods of consciousness raising. She felt like she was making progress but wasn't certain what she needed for happiness.

One day while soaking in a skin-temperature bath, she drifted into a meditative state that was different from anything she had previously experienced. She said, "All the things I thought were me—ideas about background, family, and jobs—started dropping away, one by one. Yet I was still there after the ideas I had thought were me were gone. I felt changed but undiminished, ready to live my life with a freedom that I'd never felt or known before. I had dropped all the misconceptions about myself that I'd been carrying around for years like excess baggage. The main thing I needed for happiness was getting acquainted with myself."

Life offers choices on a continuing basis. Knowledge of the self leads to better decision making and consequently better choices. the individual who recognizes the value to the self of being kind, fair, and responsible can make choices on that basis. Making choices may mean making mistakes, but making mistakes is a very human action as well as an important part of experience as noted in this timeless Zen story:

The Wise Teacher's Mistakes

A wise teacher, nearing the end of a long life, was asked by a student, "What would you do differently if you were given the opportunity to relive your life?"

The teacher replied, "I'd make more mistakes."

The student asked, "Why would you do that?"

The teacher answered, "I learned more about myself from my mistakes than from any other source and self-knowledge is the most important kind."

After pondering that for a while, the student asked, "How can I learn more from my mistakes?"

"Pay attention to the experience," replied the teacher, "and it will teach you about yourself, your talents, and your abilities. Remember that every mistake means learning not to do it again and learning to forgive yourself for having made it."

In addition to teaching the individual to survive, the culture teaches the individual to make choices that insure the survival of the culture. The value of such decisions may not be to the individual but to the culture. Some individuals rebel against the entire culture when they realize this. The following story about a young rebel and a hip counselor gives a Zen perspective on rebellion:

Dues

Rebel: "I'm not going to pay those kind of dues because I don't want to be in that kind of club."

Counselor: "Sure. I know. See, I already wrote your predictable response into the record."

Rebel:"What do you mean predictable?"

Counselor: "Everybody knows you do the opposite of what is asked. That's the dues you pay for being a compulsive rebel."

Rebel: "What do you know about paying dues?"

Counselor: "Before I got hip I pissed off two dudes who hung out in some of the places I did. They started treating me like a bad dude. I reacted by acting toward them like I was a bad dude. Soon more people were treating me like a bad dude and I realized that dues for acting like a bad dude were being treated like a bad dude. I gave it up. For saying no every time someone wants a yes, your dues are being treated as predictable."

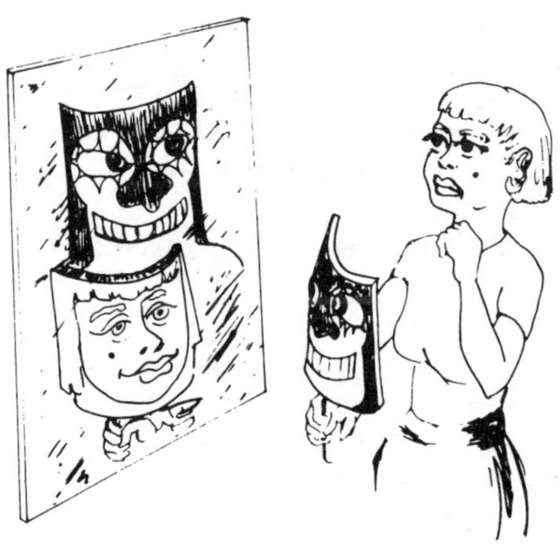

The individual who heavily invests personal identity in a temporary role may experience an identity crisis when the role is over.

The journey of self-discovery requires the individual to distinguish the self from the roles the individual plays. Many roles are temporary. The individual who heavily invests personal identity in a temporary role may experience an identity crisis when the role is over. Having self-knowledge gives the person who has lost one role the ability to take on another role without self-doubt.

Honesty is a direct route to self-knowledge. The person who practices honesty in speech and action creates a personal reality on a foundation that enhances being truthful in thought. Honesty in thought leads to personal insights regarding the nature of the self.

The following contemporary Zen story reveals the pitfalls of lying as well as the power of honesty:

Dennis's Truthtelling Group

Dennis realized that his lying was getting out of control one day when he was late getting to the office. When he got there, instead of saying he overslept, he told a long and adventurous tale about a woman from his past who had re-entered his life. When he finished his story, no one in the office said anything. Dennis asked, "What, no comments?"

Felix responded by asking, "Will all those here who believed Dennis's story please raise their right hands?"

No hands were raised.

Felix asked, "Will all those who enjoyed Dennis's story please raise their right hands?"

No hands were raised.

Felix asked, "Will all those who listened to Dennis's story please raise their right hands?"

No hands were raised.

Felix said, "Dennis, there are your comments. Not only

does no one believe your stories, no one listens anymore. The meaningful part of this episode is that you didn't raise your hand either. You have lied so much to so many that you don't enjoy, believe, or even listen to your own lies."

Dennis said, "Maybe I should start a Liars Anonymous Group."

Felix said, "Call it the Truthtellers Group. Ex-liars need a positive image."

Dennis said, "I'll do it. I'm going to be a truthteller."

Felix replied, "Why don't you start here in the office by telling us your legal name? Most of us know that it isn't Dennis."

Honesty leads to self-knowledge in different ways for different individuals. When a person starts being honest about what he or she knows, believes, feels, does, and thinks, that person is directly experiencing personal reality, the reality of the self.

Honesty reduces fear as the acceptance of what exists increases. The fear of the unknown is diminished in the person who can deal honestly with the known as it emerges from the unknown.

For many individuals who are trapped in a fast paced life that fails to satisfy, honesty can be a way of diminishing the hurry habit. As honesty produces greater self-knowledge, the person can drop the activities that did little for the self and merely served to validate the thoughts about the ego.

Honesty causes the individual to take responsibility for the personal reality in which he or she lives. External reality provides input to the person. The mind of the person interprets the input to experience a personal reality. Acceptance of the position of being the co-creator of reality is an honest recognition of the power of the self.

Life is a journey of self-discovery. Each step makes future steps easier.

OPTIONAL EXERCISES

1. Journal Entry

Write Your own obituary as it might be submitted to your local newspaper today. Realize that it will be edited to contain just the facts before it is published. Write in your journal any self-knowledge that this entry produced.

2. Forgiveness Exercise

If there is a mistake that you have made that is currently bothering you, use the following procedure:

A. Admit to yourself and to the necessary others that you made a mistake.

B. Do what you can to rectify any damage caused by the mistake.

C. Review what you've learned from the mistake including learning how not to make a similar mistake again.

D. Forgive yourself for making the mistake.

E. Give yourself approval for using this procedure for mistake closure.

3. Slowing Down Exercise

If you are caught in the hurry habit, slow down. Rearrange your life so you have some time for yourself and self-knowledge.

4. Self-awareness Exercise

Whenever you become aware that your mind has taken a leave of absence from your body and is focused elsewhere, bring your attention back to your body to increase awareness that the self-knowledge of the body is important.

5. Spontaneous Exercise

If your life lacks spontaneity, plan for spontaneity by leaving some time in your schedule to do something enjoyable that is not scheduled or pre-planned.

CHAPTER 12

The Zen of Complete Views

The first aspect of Buddha's eightfold path leading to the end of frustration and suffering is complete views. Complete views are the liberated views that a person develops by following the eightfold path. The yin and yang of complete views are self-knowledge and world knowledge.

Understanding is the essence of complete views. When a person understands that the ego is not the self, that person is progressing toward liberation from the egocentric lifestyle. The pitfalls of ego-oriented living are many. The following excerpt from one of Otis's Zen talks identifies the main problem with ego-oriented living:

Hanging Up the Ego

"Your ego will hang you up if you don't know who you are. The desires of the ego are not based on reality. If you let your ego convince you that you want everyone to like you, you'll lose sight of your own reality trying to be likable in all the separate realities of others. If you acted like the most likable person in the world and got a lot of people to buy your act, that wouldn't be as important as learning to like yourself.

"Treat your ego like a garment you don't need to wear. Hang it up so it won't hang you up. The desires of the ego are imaginary and can't be satisfied. No matter what you chase to satisfy the ego—money, pleasure, fame, luxuries—you are doomed to fail with that shortsighted view. No matter how much you get, you'll still have to learn that when trying to satisfy the ego too much is never enough."

After the ego has been recognized as a construct of the mind, self-discovery follows. Dropping all the actions and thoughts related to ego satisfaction is a direct result of changing the limited ego views to more complete views. Replacing those thoughts and actions with honesty is a key to updating complete views as revealed in this introduction to the Truthtellers Group:

Paul's Truthteller Group

"Welcome. If you have been telling lies and want to tell the truth, you've come to the right place. My name is Paul. Some of you may know me as Dennis. That was a name I formerly used to avoid finding out who Paul is. Admitting my identity was my first step in discovering myself through honesty.

"Honesty is an undervalued technique in dealing with reality. For years, I lied to everyone. I looked upon telling the truth as a failure of the creative imagination. I used lies to make other people think I was the most interesting character they ever met. It was fun for a while until I realized that aware people saw through my lies and considered me a fool for lying to them. So I limited my associations a bit and spent most of my time with those who believed me. Then I realized that I was wasting my time spending it with people I didn't respect. The reason I didn't respect them was because they believed me. My lies had me locked into a losing lifestyle.

"So I took up honesty as a technique to end my frustration. I used honesty to reveal myself, not as a means to hurt others. And it worked. My life started getting better and I discovered my relationships improved. Being honest means you don't have to remember what you said and you don't have to remember who you said it to."

Self-knowledge and world knowledge both come from experience. As the ancient Taoists observed nature to learn the ways of the world, the Zenist or Zen-oriented person observes experience as a natural process in the world, knowing that the observer is not separate form whatever is observed. Observation leads to understanding; understanding makes views more complete.

Observation of personal experience should be internal as well as external and include awareness of the body, sensations, thoughts, and mental processes. Personal observation tells the observer as much about the way the observer's mind works as about the way the world works. The following contemporary Zen story demonstrates the importance of observing and knowing the workings of the mind:

The Dirty Game

When Judy lived alone for the first time in her life, she discovered that she had no one to blame for the unhappiness she felt. Previously, she had always attributed her suffering to the actions of others. When there was no one but herself to hold responsible, she realized she needed help and joined a self-help group.

Within the group, she did her best to be honest about her behavior, her goals, and her reality. Another member of the group gave Judy the insight she needed to have a happier life by saying, "Judy, you are playing a dirty game with yourself. You judge yourself by shifting standards. If you act spontaneously and don't like the results, you think, 'I should have looked before I leaped.' If you take time to plan actions and you don't like the results, you think, 'I lost because I hesitated.' Neither of those statements applies all the time. You judge yourself by hindsight and

> always find yourself guilty. You set high standards for everything you attempt. If you don't meet those standards, you are unhappy. If you do meet those standards, instead of feeling good about it you respond by raising the standards, telling yourself that you didn't expect enough of yourself. You've set things up so that no matter what happens, you lose. Why don't you stop playing games with yourself that you can't win?"

Judy suffered from having a poor opinion of herself based on her opinion that she should be perfect. She created her own suffering and frustration because her incomplete views didn't distinguish between opinions and knowledge.

Observing of the experience of others requires the same critical attention as observing personal experience. The person who is able to analyze the experience of others in relation to himself or herself develops a greater awareness of the differences in personal realities.

One teacher explained differing realities to her students in terms of the test they were to take. She said, "The test questions I write on the blackboard reflect my personal reality; those are the questions I believe will test your knowledge of the subject. Your response to those questions is your personal reality and it is written evidence that each one of us lives in a personal reality that differs from all other personal realities. My questions and your answers are objective reality that can be independently verified. The objective reality that all the answers are not identical verifies that each of us is living in a separate reality."

Observing the experience of others helps the observer develop empathy and a greater opportunity for learning vicariously. Liberation requires that each individual find the truth for himself or herself. Those who learn from someone else's experience are free to make their own mistakes instead of repeating the mistakes of others.

Reflection on the results of observation and analysis provides insight. Insight is relief from individual misunderstanding. Relief from misunderstanding creates changes in behavior and experience. These changes are then subject to observation, analysis, and reflection to be included in the new and improved complete views.

An understanding that everything changes is basic to complete views. Everything that exists is the moving Tao. The movement is change. Survival is living with the changes. Complete views help produce the flexibility, adaptability, and versatility of liberation; these characteristics are more important to survival than fitness.

Most cultures treat survival as a serious business. But the culture is more interested in cultural survival than individual survival. Breaking the cultural trance allows an individual to develop more complete views than the limited views of cultural institutions.

Achieving more complete views complements the cultural seriousness with an understanding of the humorous aspects of the human condition. As Jo the Joker said, "If you can't laugh at yourself, you're missing an important part of the experience of feeling completely alive. I would rather feel completely alive than know the meaning of life."

The following Zen sermon from Buddy Darma emphasizes that a sense of humor helps develop complete views:

The Darma Karma Theory

From my own experience I've developed a theory of karma. I believe that if you can't understand someone else's experience, you will have an experience similar to that person's experience. That's an important part of karma as I understand it.

For instance, I had friends with ulcers but I never understood ulcers until I got one. Like Phil Dick said, "Reality denied comes back to haunt." Ulcers haunted me until I got rid of my egocentric view of experience. That ego love habit can be broken. I'll tell you the five steps that worked for me. Feel free to use them if you need them:

The ego love habit can be broken.

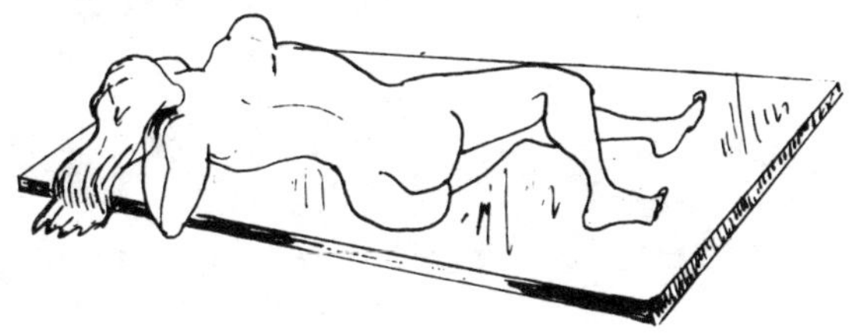

1. Stop sleeping on full length mirrors.

2. Wear very ordinary clothes.

3. Cease acquiring love slaves.

4. Explore ego-baffling experiences.

5. Stop dressing up to masturbate.

OPTIONAL EXERCISES

1. Journal Entry

Write a brief summary of one of the experiences you have had that helped you have more complete views.

2. Serious Exercise

Make a serious effort to put more laughter and amusement in your life. Read funny books. Listen to comics. Watch more comedies. Discover things that make you laugh. Keep doing this until you can no longer take this exercise seriously.

3. Boredom Exercise

The next time you seem bored, take responsibility for your own boredom. Do this by focusing on what you should be doing and do it. Repetition of this exercise will help develop complete views.

4. Spontaneity Exercise

Invent and perform your own spontaneous exercise. You can be sure it is spontaneous if you act without ego involvement.

5. View Exercise

Listen to other people's point of view. Compare it to your own. Examine the differences and determine which are based on knowledge and which are based on opinion.

CHAPTER 13

The Zen of Right Intentions

The second aspect of Buddha's eightfold path leading to the end of frustration and suffering is right intentions. Right intentions are based on complete views. As a person's views become more complete, the intentions of that person can become much more right. Right intentions are an attitude of good will toward the Tao, everything that exists including the self.

As a person's views become more complete, the intentions of that person can become much more right.

The following story form the 1970s points to the power of right intentions:

Horizontal Management

A technical writer was asked by a former coworker if he was interested in writing a user's manual for a new computer company. The writer said he was interested. The former coworker said, "Good. I called you because the company prefers to hire people that current employees recommend as someone who can do the job and is a conscientious worker."

The writer was interviewed by the people he would be working with and by the president. All of them seemed interested in their jobs and in helping the writer obtain the information needed to create a useful manual. A few days later he was offered the job and accepted.

When the writer reported for work, the president showed him his office. He asked the president to whom he should report. The president said, "We have periodic meetings where you report problems and progress. We operate on the horizontal rather than the vertical management theory. Managers are service personnel. They service the workers. The office manager will come by your office now and then to see if there is anything you need to do your work. We've learned that people who are interested in doing the work don't need constant supervision so we save money on management expense by hiring people who have the right intentions."

The good will of right intentions does not mean ignoring personal experience. The attitude of good will must incorporate experience so that the individual does not repeat mistakes. If one individual finds that he or she is suffering because another particular individual has taken advantage of his or her good will, then it is the responsibility of the first person to find the right intentions so that suffering is not repeated. This can be achieved by updating complete views and right intentions as beliefs and illusions fade.

Vance Bourjaily had a character in one of his novels say that as many people lose illusions, they gain defenses and mistake the process for spiritual growth. From a Zen perspective, lost illusions are replaced with a greater knowledge of the world. This greater knowledge can be used for spiritual growth when incorporated into views and intentions. Before creating any defense, the Zen-oriented person tends to question what is being defended and what is it being defended against. Frequently the answer is the ego is being defended. Since the ego doesn't exist when not thought about, it needs no defense. Often the defense would be against the loss of a cherished idea that is limiting the development of right intentions.

Right intentions reduce frustration and suffering for the person who has those intentions and for those who encounter that person. The person with right intentions decreases victimization by not making victims of others or the self. The power of right intentions makes the individual life path more harmonious.

Each individual is a unique combination of traits and abilities. Personal experience teaches most people that those traits and abilities are not important in themselves, that what is important is the use made of these characteristics. Right intentions forecast the best potential usage. For the Zen-oriented person on Buddha's path, right intentions are using personal characteristics to reduce frustration and suffering for the self and for others.

The following story of right intentions is also a tale of self-discovery:

The Zen of Selling

When George finished school he took a job as a salesperson. He enjoyed talking with the customers, finding out what they wanted, and meeting their needs as best he could. After a short time he realized that he was never going to be the top money-making salesperson on the staff. To achieve that required hard selling based on getting the maximum that the customer could pay.

George's right intentions were not appreciated at work. He began planning to find another place of employment. His first step was to start saving money so he'd have greater economic choices. His next step was to look for a job where the customers were never treated as potential victims.

Eventually George bought a bookstore. There he talked with the customers, learned their wants, and stocked his store accordingly. His motto, "Every transaction is a bargain for both buyer and seller," is his Zen of selling, using abilities with right intentions.

Prejudice, an adverse opinion based on insufficient and limited knowledge, is a major obstacle to achieving right intentions. The prejudiced person frequently develops prejudice through: 1. Believing that his or her personal characteristics and accidents of birth are so important that anyone who doesn't have them is inferior; 2. Believing that real or perceived action, beliefs, or characteristics of a small sample of members of an apparently identifiable group are undesirable and are common to all members of that group. Both of these methods of developing prejudice are examples of ignorance in action, a failure to understand experience, a lack of knowledgeable views, a shortage of right intentions.

Because prejudiced individuals live in a personal reality where they confuse their beliefs with knowledge, they often present their opinion as if it were an objective fact. Some combine ignorance with arrogance and demand that their prejudices be respected by others. The person with right intentions can avoid endorsing ignorance. Sometimes, as in the following story, right intentions can defeat prejudiced intentions.

The Blackball of Prejudice

In the 1950s at Georgia Tech at a fraternity membership meeting, Sid spoke in favor of Joe, his high school friend, who was to be voted on that evening. Several other members spoke highly of Joe. No one had anything adverse to say about Joe, so the leather bag was circulated and each member put in a white marble for a yes vote or a black marble for a no vote.

The bag was opened. all the marbles were white except one. Joe had been blackballed and membership would be denied.

Sid said, "No one spoke of any opposition to Joe. Would the member who voted against him please identify himself?"

The blackballing member did.

Sid said, "If you have anything against Joe other than his Chinese ancestry, I'd like to hear about it."

The blackballing member replied, "Nothing else."

Sid responded, "This fraternity was founded about a hundred years ago with no racial or religious restrictions against membership. I joined this fraternity because it was an unprejudiced organization. Now that prejudice has been introduced, let's take prejudice all the way to the end and see what that end will be. If Joe is denied membership because of prejudice, then I will blackball every future potential member of this fraternity to protect them from exposure to prejudice. I'm a freshman. If I blackball every

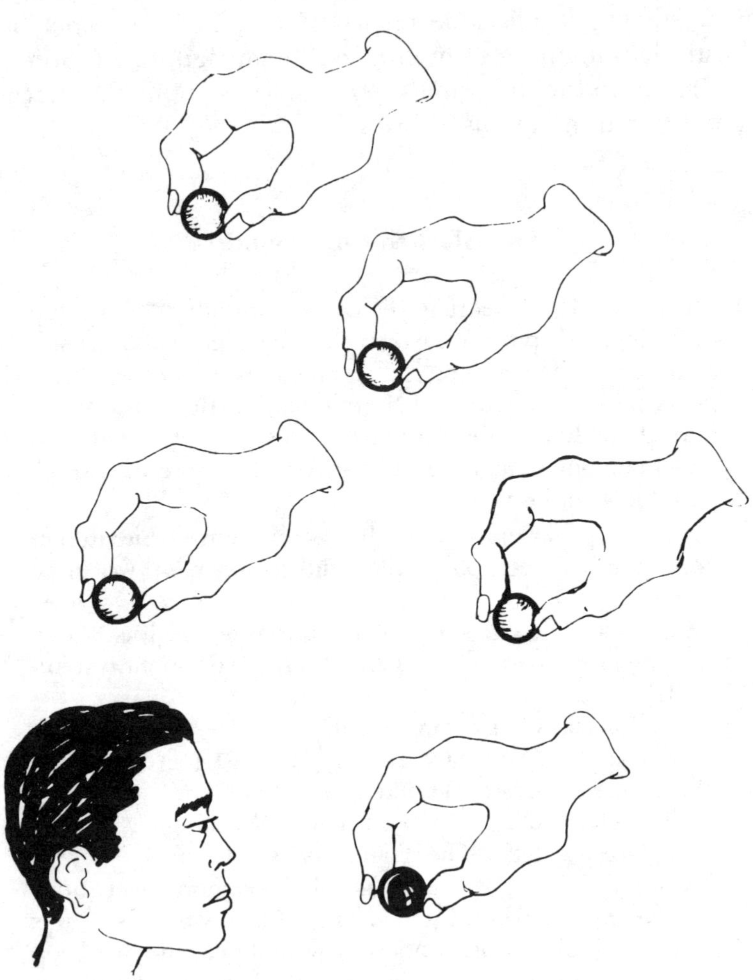

> person proposed for membership, this fraternity will die for lack of new members before I graduate. All of you know me well enough to know I carry out my intentions when I'm sure I'm right. I'm willing to fight prejudice until death—the death of this fraternity chapter. Does anyone have anything else to say before I call for a second vote on Joe?"
>
> Joe became a member and later became one of the most popular fraternity presidents on campus. Sid became a role model for members interested in good intentions.

In the preceding story, the prejudiced member was confronted with the reality that his bigotry would destroy what he wanted to preserve if he acted from prejudiced intentions. He saw clearly that he would become a victim of his own prejudice.

An important part of the truth about prejudice is that a prejudiced intention is a detriment and disadvantage to the person having it. Bigots are often so concerned with the group they hate that they miss the significance of their own lives. As Discordian Ms. Nancy Fancymanners said, "I know prejudice is stupid, but I just can't help it. I admit it. I am prejudiced against prejudiced people and I don't associate with them. Of course, I don't have to. No one invites them anywhere important."

The development of right intentions requires updating as personal experience produces more information about current reality. The Tao is constantly moving and the aware person of right intentions moves in harmony with it. Right intentions require learning from the past and changing past intentions to present intentions. As Ralph said, "When I was a kid, I wanted an electric train set. I didn't get one. I could buy an electric train now but that kid that I was isn't around anymore to give it to. I used to relive the frustration that kid felt every time I saw an electric train. So I bought one. I gave it away because I'm not that kid anymore and I decided that kissing that ass of the past is no way to live."

OPTIONAL EXERCISES

1. Journal Entry

Write in your journal about the relationship between complete views and right intentions.

2. Good Will Exercise

Spend one day showing good will toward the world. Try to make ever interaction a pleasant one. Summarize your day in the journal. Pay particular attention to the changes in mood you experience and how you can use that information.

3. Intentions Exercise

Look for evidence that there is a conspiracy that intends to provide you with the answers you need. You can consider this book part of the conspiracy.

4. Prejudice Exercise

Examine your own intentions thoroughly for prejudice. When you find prejudice, examine how it causes frustration and suffering in others. Then examine how it causes frustration and suffering in your life.

5. Humorous Intentions Exercise

Find a way to incorporate humor in your intentions. You should have a sense of humor about your intentions to help you when they change.

CHAPTER 14

The Zen of Action

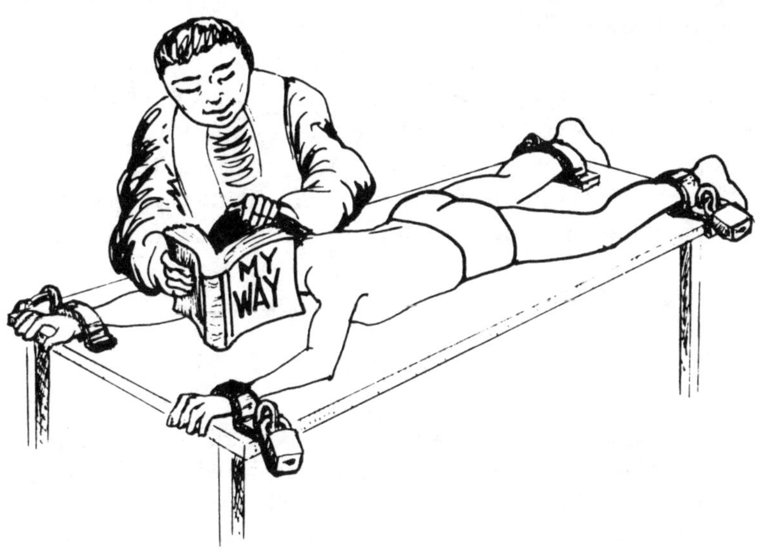

Requiring or expecting others to have your morals is the height of immorality.

The next five aspects of Buddha's eightfold path—truthful speech, correct conduct, appropriate vocation, earnest effort, and continuing alertness—are about action, behavior in the world. Buddha spoke of these behaviors not to impose any abstract code of morals on anyone but as a way for any individual to combat frustration and suffering. As Reverend Dr. Resident said, "Your morals are for you alone. Requiring or expecting others to have your morals is the height of immorality."

The Zen-oriented person acts from the inside out, making actor and action a unity. Behavior is based on views and intentions. With complete views and right intentions, action is the self moving in harmony with the Tao; behavior is the expression of the self. The Zenist's behavioral freedom extends to all actions for which he or she will accept responsibility.

The Zen of truthful speech, devoid of lies, slander and abuse, is useful for self-discovery. As Paul the Truthteller said, "When I called myself Dennis, I thought that I was hiding my identity from others. I learned that I was preventing myself from learning who Paul is. I got tired of living with a stranger." But the truth must be used with discretion as indicated in this Zen story:

Ed's Truth

In the first week on a new job as technical editor for a large industrial firm, Ed's supervisor asked him his opinion of a memorandum the supervisor had written. Ed said that it needed work. The supervisor asked him to mark the necessary changes on the memorandum and bring it back to him. Ed did so and then went back to his major task, editing a company report.

During the rest of the week, the supervisor kept interrupting Ed, asking Ed to justify with an authoritative reference each of the many changes Ed had indicated in the memorandum. Ed took the time to do it.

On Monday, Ed's supervisor criticized him because the company report wasn't finished. Then he read to Ed another poorly prepared memorandum. He asked Ed what he thought of it. Ed replied, "I think you have expressed the situation exactly as you perceive it."

The Zen of correct conduct is behaving in accordance with right intentions. Conduct that is in keeping with intentions gives greater meaning to personal experience.

Behavior that represents the self in action is often a factor in feeling completely alive. As Tao Jones said, "Moving with the Tao is an effortless way of keeping up with the self."

Correct conduct for the Zenist is not based on abstract or idealized concepts but on understanding the Zen of Buddha's path. One person's ideal behavior may be another person's concept of wretched excess. Each person has a separate reality that shapes behavior. The person who doesn't know what his or her behavior means needs to pay more attention to personal conduct.

At a question and answer session after a Discordian Zen lecture, someone asked Buddy Darma how he could determine if his own conduct was correct. Buddy replied, "Just put your attention on the answers to these questions:

1. Is your conduct decent, wise, and useful?

2. Does your conduct cause you suffering?

3. Does your conduct cause others suffering?

4. Do you treat anyone as less than an equal?

5. Do you like people who behave as you do?

The Zen of appropriate vocation requires thinking about the answers to similar questions. Does the work need to be done? Will the work lessen suffering in the worker and in the world? What levels of knowledge, skill, ability, and talent are required? Will doing the work help the worker become a better person? These are not the only questions; every separate reality supplies others, as in this story:

Spending Time

Judson was the successful professional that he had labored years to become. He liked the work he was doing. He felt he was helping people. He was making more money per hour than he had ever imagined making.

Yet he felt something was wrong. Life seemed to be passing him by. He asked his friend, Shiela, what he should do. She suggested that he take a week's retreat at a health resort. He asked, "Do you know how much money I'd lose if I didn't work?" Shiela asked, "Has your time become so valuable that you can't spend any if on yourself?"

Finding suitable vocation is action that requires adapting to changing circumstances. Many people try a variety of occupations in their lifetime. Those who discover that what they are doing is an appropriate vocation are the happiest people.

The Zen of earnest effort can be a part of every action. Earnest effort is focusing on the action being performed and, using the energy created by the focus, accomplishing the act with one-pointedness of mind. Earnest effort creates a unity of mind and body, a unity of actor and action.

Zelda, of the Discordian DADA (Discordian Artists Discovering Artistry), said, "With effort, you can discover the artist within you. The Balinese say that they have no art as such—that they just do everything the best they can. That's the kind of effort many Discordians put into living because they see their lives as their art forms."

Earnest effort can be blocked by tension. One of the simple methods of dissipating tension is by moving the muscles. If the tense situation can be walked away from, the walking will reduce some of the tension. Tension can also be reduced by regular meditation, by progressive muscle relaxation, by massage, by warmth, by sexual climax, by laughter. Kokomo Dragonlady used humor in her newsletter to members of her Sex Without Partners Association; she once wrote that the tension releasing potential of masturbation was first suspected by Shakey Jake the Snakehandler who became so nervous that his every attempt at urination led to ejaculation.

Earnest effort is the route to making every action seem effortless.

Earnest effort is the route to making every action seem effortless. This apparent paradox can be observed in the action of athletes, performers, and others who become one with their actions. As Zen Showman says, "If you expend the effort to make something that appears difficult look easy, you've got yourself a good act; if you extend that to everything you do, you've got yourself a good life."

The Zen of continuing alertness is the action of attention. The classic story of attention involves an experienced mule handler, called a muleskinner, and the sale of a trained mule. The seller told the buyer what commands the mule would obey. The buyer got ready to leave, said, "Giddy-up" to make the mule move, and demanded his money back when the mule remained where it was. The seller picked up a stick, struck the mule, and shouted "Giddy-up." The mule moved. The seller said "I forgot to tell you to get his attention first."

Buddy Darma told the mule story to some of his students. After the amusement subsided, he said, "That muleskinner who hit the mule reminds me of a Zen Master who strikes his meditators. In this Discordian Zen School there are no sticks, just tricks.

"I intend to transmorgify your entire concept of Western civilization by the insidious introduction of reality into your consciousness. I'm putting my attention on getting your attention. If I fail, I will be glad to give you a diploma that certifies you are a jackass. If I succeed, you will be a Discordian Zenist with all the duties, rights, and privileges you can get away with."

All of the aspects of the eightfold path are interrelated. The ability to follow the path is enhanced by the attention of continuing alertness. The Zenist uses earnest effort to maintain alertness at a functional level. Too low a lever produces a zombie-like existence; too high a level yields tension and can crate paranoia.

Trinidad John said in his rap about paranoia: "Paranoia is the disease of the quasi-hip. Like the cat who is afraid of losing his cool always has his eyes on what could be wrong instead of just being alert to the scene, the paranoid is on a bad trip caused by a delusion of reference with a strong negative twist. The complete trip is in five stages. The paranoid's inner voice recognizes the five stages of paranoia like this:

1. I think they could be looking for me.

2. They probably are looking for me.

3. I know they are looking for me.

4. They have found me.

5. I am becoming one of them.

Trinidad John wrapped up the rap by saying, "Some paranoids get so good at this losing trip that they can't give it up; once they get through all five stages from one perspective, they shift perspectives and do it all again. Personally, I'm not bothered by paranoia anymore. When my alertness makes me aware that people are following me, I just assume that the people are talent scouts."

The five aspects of action—speech, conduct, vocation, effort, alertness—from an independent Zen point of view are guides to behavior that will diminish suffering. As Normal Zensense Spiel wrote in "The Five and Zen Sense Store Journal:" "The positive point of view in Discordian Zen turns confusion into fun, anxiety into laughter, and life into art."

OPTIONAL EXERCISES

1. Journal Entry

Write in your journal the relationships you perceive among the actions of speech, conduct, vocation, effort, and alertness.

2. Action Exercise

In some area of your conduct that you wish to change, devise an exercise that will alert you to make the effort to match conduct with intentions.

3. Vocation Exercise

In your journal write down all the vocations in which you have experience. Make a list of five other vocations for which you have the necessary qualifications.

4. Effort Exercise

Make an effort to see the humor in the fact that the joke is on you if you take your attention to the point of serious tension.

5. Anxiety Conversion Exercise

Be alert to opportunities to convert your anxiety through action into laughter.

CHAPTER 15

The Zen of Thorough Concentration

The eighth aspect of the eightfold path is thorough concentration. Concentration is one-pointedness of mind. Many Zenists practice thorough concentration in meditation, but is can be practiced in any human activity.

Some people are surprised at their inability to concentrate on meditation. One student told a meditation teacher, "I can't be quiet for 20 minutes and concentrate on my breathing. It makes me feel that I'm being pursued by unnamed fears." The teacher replied, "Don't let pursuit by unnamed fears halt your meditation. Let the unnamed fears catch up. Then you can easily give them a name if you need to. Those fears are just distracting thoughts passing through your mind; let them pass on through like any other thought. Get back to thorough concentration on your meditation. When your meditation period is over, you can concentrate on dealing with fears if that is the next thing you choose to do."

Thorough concentration is an asset to any activity. At a writers conference, one Zen-oriented writer, when discussing writer's block, said, "I use the technique of always having more than one writing project in progress. If I'm blocked on one, I work on another. I usually have something to add to another manuscript while I'm waiting for the block bypass to manifest itself. The information to overcome the block on the first manuscript usually just pops into my mind within two weeks. If I can't work on any of my writing projects, I suspect I'm having what Ted Sturgeon called a doing-things block. That's something else. I overcome that by focusing on some long overdue physical task—like straightening out my closet—and using my concentration to focus all my energy on getting it done. That makes me feel so good that I can overcome anything—even writer's block."

Concentration, like meditation, improves with practice. As with all other activities, self-knowledge helps determine the timing for concentration as indicated in this contemporary Zen story:

Forty Days to Enlightenment

At a New Age spiritual conference, recently married Felix and Zelda gave a lecture on the consciousness raising opportunities in marriage. After the lecture, one of the attendees told them that he had a 40 day procedure that produced the ultimate in consciousness raising, a genuine cosmic consciousness experience of enlightenment. Felix and Zelda seemed interested. The man said that he had derived his procedure from an esoteric, allegorical explanation of the symbolism in the tales of a flood caused by forty days of rain. He said that the first requirement was to remain celibate for 40 days to allow the kundalini energy to accumulate.

Zelda and Felix looked at each other and Zelda said, "Please give us your card for future reference. Now isn't the right time for us to concentrate on your procedure."

Thorough concentration is an aid in raising the consciousness of the person doing the concentrating. Those people who wish to raise the consciousness of others should concentrate on this message from Arthur: "Concentrating on trying to change the consciousness of enough individuals to get a majority won't get your near as far as changing the consciousness of the people who are good at thinking and communicating to the masses."

Zen Showman, in a talk on the Zen of acting, emphasized the importance form an acting standpoint of concentrating on your experience. He said, "As an actor, you must see life as a process to be experienced. If you see life as something to be endured, it's equivalent to buying a ticket, going to the theater, taking your seat, and ignoring the performance."

One of Buddy Darma's Discordian Zen School Students attempted to justify his lack of concentration on ordinary tasks by saying that he was concentrating on becoming enlightened. Buddy replied, "Enlightenment is just another experience. You can concentrate on it when it comes around. In the meantime, concentrate on what you are doing. If you aren't doing anything, concentrate on the next thing that needs to be done and do it. That's the way to improve your concentration every day and you'll feel more enlightened tomorrow than you do today."

Concentrating on the past is useful to update complete views from past action experiences. Concentrating on the suffering of the past is useful only if it provides insights that will reduce suffering in the present and future.

Sam, a Buddhist and a psychodramatist, once counseled a woman who had become suicidal from dwelling on the guilt she felt over a childhood situation. He said, "Well, there is certainly a lot of guilt in that situation. Your father has the guilt of exploiting your family loyalty. Your mother has the guilt of ignoring what was happening to you. What were you doing? You were trying to keep the family together under difficult circumstances. Where's the guilt in that? You've taken their guilt, tried to make it yours, and suffered for it. Concentrate on giving up that guilt; it doesn't belong to you."

Zenny Bruce's standup comic routine starts with him saying, "My shrink asked me if I had invisible playmates as a child. I concentrated on the question and then answered. 'No, but I used to think I had.' She asked me what I would do if I had to watch my childhood unfold all over again. I said that I'd keep my finger pressed down on the fast forward button."

As therapist Gary said, "Reliving the past without gaining insight is dumpster diving." As Ms. Nancy Fancymanners advised: "Don't grovel in your old garbage. That's as bad for you as getting all covered with dogma."

If there is a known obstacle to concentration, then concentration should be one way to overcome the obstacle as in this story:

Psychological Warfare

Roxanne was having lunch with her friend Shiela and talking about the problems she was having with her new lover. She said, "The sex is fantastic. No complaints. But he keeps me from concentrating on anything but him. I'm neglecting family, friends, and business. I'm even neglecting myself because I can't concentrate on anything but him. When I try to tell him about it, he explains everything in psychological terms but nothing changes. I've got to get rid of this guy. What can I do?"

Shiela suggested, "Tell him you've revealed everything to your therapist and she says you shouldn't see him anymore."

Thorough concentration aids in living with awareness without being preoccupied with security, sensation, and power. When one Zen teacher was asked, "Where do you find the kind of people that are written about in contemporary Zen stories?" She replied, "Concentrate on becoming one of them and you will find them everywhere."

The five aspects of action provide experience. Thorough concentration on experience provides self-knowledge and world knowledge. The increased self-knowledge and world knowledge makes views more complete and promotes development of right intentions. Right intentions are expressed in truthful speech, correct conduct, appropriate vocation, earnest effort, and continuing alertness providing the experiences to repeat another cycle.

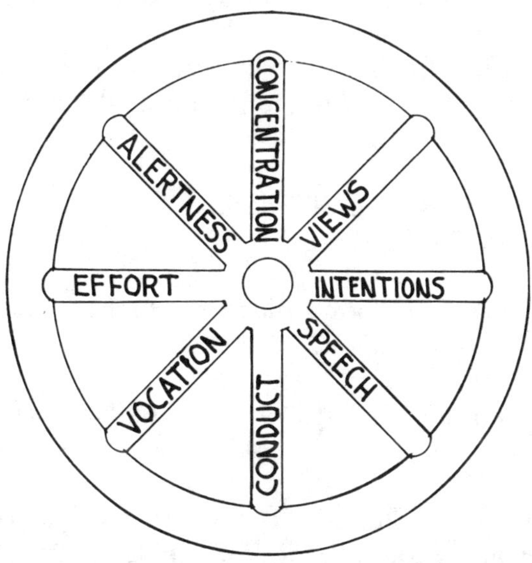

An eight-spoked wheel is often a symbol of Buddhism. The eight spokes each have a word written on them. The words are views, intentions, speech, conduct, vocation, effort, alertness, and concentration.

Thorough concentration on all aspects of the path provides the feedback for the course corrections necessary to stay on track. The Zen of following Buddha's path is like the Zen of bicycling—continuing course corrections keep you moving toward a better, more joyous life.

The joy of Zen is better experienced than described, but some descriptions, like the following, catch some of the flavor derived from the Zen of thoroughly concentrating on following Buddha's path:

"It's like dreaming about this marvelous garment you're wearing and waking up gloriously naked."—Zelda

"For me, it was finding out what the plot line really is for the role I'm playing in life's human comedy."—Zen Showman

"I invested in the Zen of Buddha's path and it's paying me dividends."—Tao Jones

"If the experience hadn't made me high, I wouldn't be known as Otis the Elevated."—Otis

"On the sensual level, following Buddha's path is like learning to make love to yourself."—Kokomo Dragonlady

"Buddha's path is like the current that helps you move gracefully along the river of life."—Huckleberry Zen

"The flavor of Zen is like the taste of tea. Take it a mouthful at a time and smile."—Ms. Nancy Fancymanners

"I learned to laugh on Buddha's path."—Zenny Bruce

"Following the Zen of Buddha's path hasn't made me love everybody but it has helped me deliver a lascivious treat to every body I selected for love."—Hazel the Hipster

OPTIONAL EXERCISES

1. Journal Entry

Write in your journal how you expect to benefit if you follow Buddha's path.

2. Drawing Exercise

Draw or trace an image of an eight-spoked wheel and label the eight spokes.

3. Paraphrasing Exercise

Reread the quotes in this chapter. Rewrite one of them into a quote that expresses your personal experience in that area. Is your paraphrased quote fun to read? If it isn't, do something to enable you to get more fun out of your life.

4. Physical Meditation Exercise

Select some physical task that you are capable of doing, preferably one you've been delaying doing. Focus on it as if it had been assigned to you as meditation designed to raise your consciousness. Do the task with thorough concentration. Write about the experience in your journal.

5. Thorough Concentration Exercise

Thoroughly concentrate on finding things in your own development that are funny to think about or relate to other interested people. Concentrate on developing and exploring your own sense of humor.

CHAPTER 16

The Future of Zen

The timelessness and universality of the teachings of Zen Buddhism are an assurance of the future of Zen. There are always human beings interested in a way of liberation. The information explosion in this century continues to make Zen more accessible to all who are interested. Some will elect to make a formal study of Zen at a Zen Center; many will choose to follow a more independent approach to Zen.

Established Zen institutions will function in the future much as they have in the past, making the inevitable changes and making sure the institutions survive and the hierarchy continues. The independent Zenists will find a future of more independent Zen sources, more books, more lectures, more informal teachers, more people interested in Zen and willing to share their experience and their laughter.

A major reason why future interest in Zen will increase is the Zen focus on the present. Zenists consider the past useful to the extent that past experiences are understood. The future of a Zen orientation is a greater ability to focus on the experience of the present as a guide to liberation.

Zen is self-liberation of the self. Just as Buddha recognized the problems of suffering before he discovered the liberating eightfold path, the Zen student must recognize the self in order to liberate the self from ego demands, from cultural trance demands, from affectedness, and from self-consciousness. This process of liberation produces the naturalness considered to be a characteristic of

Zen. This naturalness is the Buddhahood of the free-spirited self.

For those who feel a persistent urge to look within and improve perceptions, adopting a Zen outlook on the following of Buddha's eightfold path is a practical way of living in the present and in the future. There is no requirement to abandon old beliefs or to accept any new beliefs on faith. Neither meditation not following Buddha's path requires embracing a set of beliefs. They are processes that can be tried to see if they yield benefits without unwanted sacrifices. The procedures of both enable the practitioner to replace outmoded beliefs with knowledge gained from experience.

The Zen one-pointedness of mind enables a person to recognize himself or herself as the arbitrator of personal reality and the co-creator of experience. The Zenist accepts responsibility for the experience of his or her actions and reactions. Reality is perceived as a construction created by the interaction of the observer and the observed. This reality and its future from a Zenist-Taoist viewpoint are dependent on probability rather than necessity because the Tao is not planning the next movement, it just keeps moving.

There is little dogma in Zen. Instead the emphasis is on insight. The insight is reflected in future behavior, the Zen of acting from the inside out, expressing the discovered self. This acting in the ever present now frees the actor to experience the future as it becomes the present.

The process of Zen is becoming one with experience. This is done by developing one-pointedness of mind so undivided attention can be turned to experience. As the Zenist learns from experience, egocentric behavior changes and banishes that nagging feeling that something has been left undone.

The way of Zen is demanding less and accepting more.

As a Zenist recognizes that every person has a personal reality, he or she performs fewer actions to validate one reality in terms of another's reality. By not being invested in establishing a belief in a universal reality for all, the Zenist accepts more of the available spectrum of reality.

The practice of Zen, especially independent Zen, requires little or no monetary expense with a potentially large increase in the daily quality of life. The result of the practice is the creation of a personally verified operating manual to be used for guiding the life of the creator. With reasonable maintenance, the manual can last a lifetime, valid for one very personalized future.

Although from a Zen point of view the most important day is always today, the future is perceived as the Tao's unfailing ability to renew the now being experienced. The Zenist's world knowledge predicts constant change with the renewing future. The Zenists self-knowledge makes coping with the changes a source of future spiritual growth.

The Zen of following Buddha's eightfold path will probably be adopted by more people in the near future who see it as:

1. A practical approach to lessening suffering
2. A way of developing personal behavior that reflects personal morals
3. A method of discovering the self
4. A guide to creative expression of individuality
5. A means of living in the present and being prepared for the future
6. A key to unlock the meaning of experience
7. A joyful aid to sharing laughter.

The future of sharing the laughter of Zen can be appreciated now with the stories, koans, anecdotes, and quotes of contemporary independent Zenists. The following story emphasizes keeping the ability to laugh at yourself:

Dr. Don's White Hair

At a party where he was celebrating getting his doctorate in psychology, Don was flirting with a woman he had just met who was less than half his age. When she, eying his white hair, asked him how old he was, he evaded the question. Felix overheard the conversation and later asked Don, "Do you think that evading age questions will enable you to retain the shallowness of youth?" Don replied, "Don't take it that seriously, Felix. It's just a manifestation of my immaturity."

The Zen viewpoint can be effectively used in humorous replies to argumentative questions as in this Zen story of the late 1980s:

Otis's Zen Trick

In the question and answer session after a Zen lecture, Otis was asked, "Isn't Zen all a trick?" Otis responded, "I got tricked into studying Zen by Genghis Koan. He kept hanging me up with Zen koans until I wanted answers. I found them, but I was tricked into it. So Zen is a trick if you look at it that way. Any more trick questions?"

Genghis Koan's latest koan about future goals asks, "Why hurry constantly when your destination is yourself?" He admits that it is an attempt to trick people into suspecting that the calm effectiveness found in Zenists comes from the journey of self-discovery. He says, "That's when you learn the trick of being able to laugh at yourself." Ms. Nancy Fancymanners expresses this humorous truth as, "Always, by your manner, invite others to laugh with you at your humorous mistakes. The invitations cost nothing."

Contemporary culture offers unintentional samples of the humor of Zen. In "Sullivan's Travels," a 1941 motion picture now shown on television, the major character is a film director. He is tired of making fluff films and decides to experience serious life so he can do a serious film about what he learns. After a series of misadventures including poverty and prison, he returns to Hollywood to resume his career. His experiences have convinced him that he should direct comedies. In addition to seeing the humor in the director's change of direction, Zenists see in the film the Taoist concept of the union of opposites and the Zen concept of turning anxiety into laughter.

The timelessness of Zen humor will continue into the future. Raising consciousness through wit and laughter is a technique often used in Zen. The future of this technique will be based on present examples like these:

"When you forget about when,
You enter the now of Zen."—Edgar Allan Poet

"Keep your sense of humor working. Zen is too important to be taken seriously."—Zen Showman

"One of my therapy clients said that society was so terrible that he just couldn't adjust to it. I told him that he didn't have to adjust to it. He just has to accept it for exactly what it is."—Sam

"My shrink wanted me to relive and resuffer the past. I told her I wasn't into self-abuse."—Zenny Bruce

"Try to have several good laughs every day, even if they're on you."—Shiela

"Opinions are no important except to the person emotionally dependent on his or her opinions. I think that taking your opinions too seriously handicaps, warps, and erodes your sense of humor. But that's just my opinion. You don't have to take it seriously."—Buddy Darma

"If the eightfold path seems a long journey, let laughter expand the short viewpoint."—Kokomo Dragonlady

"I've tried liberation schemes that take different approaches. Some scare you almost to death so you can feel good when they tell you there's only one way to live. Some make you pay for the experience of being attacked and then charge you more money for a pep talk to make you feel decent again. Some destroy your belief system and then fill you full of dogma. All of them made me feel punchy except Zen. The humor of Zen let me replace that punchy feeling with punch lines."—Huckleberry Zen

"If you knew what gurus knew, would you do what gurus do?"—Genghis Koan

"You don't have to be the person that your hostess or host expects you to be or even the person they want you to be. Your only requirement is to be your polite self. If they won't let you do that, excuse yourself saying that you've been suddenly taken ill. Don't overdo the suspicious look that indicates it must have been something they served."—Ms. Nancy Fancymanners

"I was going to start a new religion and grant myself absolution until I discovered Zen and learned to laugh at the past by living in the present. I'm going to write a humorous article about it. I think I'll call it 'Now and Zen.'—Professor Graybeard

"When we disagree, you can be sure that only one of us is wrong."—Buddy Darma and Otis Gibson, directors of the Discordian Zen Institute.

In the past many Westerners have mistakenly assumed that Buddhism has a pessimistic outlook because it begins with the recognition of the existence of suffering. Buddhism would be pessimistic if it stopped there. But it starts there and continues, describing the eightfold path that leads away from frustration and suffering. An understanding of the implications of following the path leads to a recognition of what could be called the optimism of Buddhism, a means of ending suffering.

Zen has always been a direct approach to Buddha's teachings, a way of getting to the essence of Buddhism and to the essence of the self. In the future, more individuals will have the opportunity to take the Zen approach to the eightfold path, where every step is away from frustration and suffering and toward ease and joy.

END

ABOUT THE AUTHOR

Camden Benares is a freelance writer and editor who has been an independent student of Zen most of his adult life. He is the author of "Zen Without Zen Masters" (Falcon Press, 1985). Camden and his wife live in Los Angeles.

ISHTAR RISING

By Robert Anton Wilson

"The Return of the Goddess. Look to Bob for the new slant on this dangerous topic."

SEX AND DRUGS

By Robert Anton Wilson

Originally by Playboy, this is a book to be enjoyed on many levels. A fine biography of an era.

PROMETHEUS RISING

By Robert Anton Wilson

Readers have been known to get angry, cry, laugh and even change their entire lives. A very dangerous book.

REVOLUTION, REBELLIOUSNESS, AND RELIGIOUSNESS

Osho Rajneesh

One of the last books before his death, New Falcon Publications is honored to be entrusted with the writings of this controversial and right-on Master of the Tantrik Path. "Rebellion has something to do with changing your consciousness, your silence, your being. It is a spiritual metamorphosis."

SECRETS OF WESTERN TANTRA

The Sexuality of the Middle Path

Christopher S. Hyatt, Ph.D.

Introduced by J. Marvin Spielgelman Ph.D.,
Preface by Robert Anton Wilson Ph.D.

Dr. Hyatt reveals for the secret methods for achieving enlightenment by the transmutation of the *orgastic reflex*. This book is user friendly and contains actual practices.

Nothing is left to the imagination. Included are methods for creating the Magickal Child using the Tarot and sexual practices.

BREAKTHROUGH BOOK OF THE 21st CENTURY!

UNDOING YOURSELF

With Energized Meditation and Other Devices

By Christopher S. Hyatt, Ph.D.

Introduced by Israel Regardie; Preface by Robert Anton Wilson; with additional material by Baron von Gundlach and Antero Alli.

Considered to be one of the most honest and powerful books ever published. Now in its 4th printing including never revealed methods of Western Tantra and the Order of the White Lion.

A MODERN SHAMAN'S GUIDE TO A PREGNANT UNIVERSE

by Christopher S. Hyatt, Ph.D. & Antero Alli

Urban Cyber-Shamans cannot afford the luxury of being victims. This practical modern guidebook will take you through the steps necessary for Regaining Your Power and Repossessing YourSelf!

THE TREE OF LIES

Clearing Out Your Mind and Filling It With Yourself:

by Christopher S. Hyatt, Ph.D.

A Book of Horror - Since It Will Change You! The latest from the mad doctor himself! Hyatt picks up where Frankenstein left off! Includes exercises. This is a completely new and original work designed to free the consciousness from the shackles of the post industrial revolution straight jacketed trance, for entrance into the alive PRESENT.

ANGEL TECH:
A Modern Shaman's Guide to Reality Selection
By Antero Alli

An access guide for the realization of the Multidimensional Self, it is also a workbook for an Invisible Institute of Higher Learning where Teachers walk amidst our daily lives ready to share the appropriate education towards our inevitable graduation. These Teachers appear direct from The No Coincidences Dept. and, **these Teachers are Us.**

ALL RITES REVERSED?!:
Ritual Technology for Self-Initiation
By Antero Alli

Ritual techniques are now brought together stripped of religious dogma and imposed beliefs, providing the means to design, and execute *Effective Ceremony*. Featuring interviews with adepts Jose Arguelles (*Mayan Factor*), Christopher S.Hyatt, Ph.D. (*Golden Dawn*), and Elizabeth Cogburn (*Shamanistic Qabalism*); plus Geomancy, Earth Surrender Rites, Dreamtime Rituals, Temple Construction, Potential Dangers and the Right Use of Will.

THE AKASHIC RECORD PLAYER:
A Non-Stop Geomantic Conspiracy
By Antero Alli

Between Boulder, Colorado and Bali . . . a man and woman meet to perform a mysterious ritual having *nothing* to do with Falling in Love, Getting Married, Having Babies and /or Buying Furniture.

NEUROPOLITIQUE
(A New Vision of Neuropolitics)
By Timothy Leary

Tom Dylan is on the loose, even in the Hole at Folsom, which just shows to go ya that ya can't keep a good Cyber-Shaman down. Now he's selling H.O. M.E.s (High-Orbital-Mini-Earths) and monitoring (of course) the mutation of an entire race.

INFO-PSYCHOLOGY
(A ReVision of Exo-Psychology)
By Timothy Leary

Don't just smile: SMI^{2}LE! You'll discover how with this manual on the use of the Human Nervous System according to the instructions of the Manufacturers.

NEURO-GENIC HYPNOSIS
A Key to the Fountain of Youth
Marco Allison, Ph.D., Robert Anton Wilson, Ph.D. and Marion Greenberg

This book explores the new discoveries in psychobiological hypnosis and its relationship to reprogramming the lower brain centers, complete with numerous techniques for self-development. Issues explored are aging, anxiety, fear, high arousal, and the bio-sexual response.

BUT NAMES WILL NEVER HURT ME
Psychological Abuse: The Effects of a Toxic Culture
Marco Allison, Ph.D., Linda Allison, BSN, et al

Our culture is a psychologically abusive culture whose ramifications are particularly noticeable in child rearing. The effects of this carry over as well to our marriages, jobs, politics and all other human relationships. Our society is therefore rife with violence, and drug addiction as an escape from the pain of maladjustment.

COMPASSION AND CONFRONTATION IN PSYCHOTHERAPY
The New Therapy for the 21st Century
Marco Allison, Ph.D., Angus Morrison M.S. and Lauren Levine M.S.

This book explores the issues of the changes in psychotherapy as we move into the 21st Century. It explores the therapeutic values of compassion, empathy as healing techniques, versus the *technician* approach that has dominated the field since Freud.

SUFISM, ISLAM AND JUNGIAN PSYCHOLOGY

By J. Marvin Spiegelman, Ph.D.
and Pir Vilayat Khan

This unique study of the Sufi doctrine analysed within a Jungian context is co-authored by Pir Vilayat Khan, the Head of the Sufi Order in the West. He is the best known and most respected English speaking Sufi Teacher. His message has reached tens of thousands of lives throughout the world.

THE COMPLETE GOLDEN DAWN SYSTEM OF MAGIC

by Israel Regardie

Israel Regardie's final testament to the Golden Dawn, a hard-bound, 1112 page, 8 x 11 volume beautifully illustrated with full-color plates. Now in its third printing, the COMPLETE Golden Dawn System of Magic is just that—complete, and considered by most students, the easiest edition to study

WHAT YOU SHOULD KNOW ABOUT THE GOLDEN DAWN

by Israel Regardie

With a Foreword by Christopher S. Hyatt

Now in its fifth, revised and enlarged printing, this is a highly personal version of Regardie's life-long experience with the forces influencing the development of modern Occultism. It contains much new information, presented by some of the most influential figures of the movement.

The SECRET INNER ORDER RITUALS OF THE GOLDEN DAWN

With the approval of Israel Regardie

By Patrick J. Zalewski

Edited by Joseph Lisiewski

Any Golden Dawn library is incomplete without this volume of never-before-published information form Golden Dawn archives. Zalewski, Israel Regardie and Christopher S. Hyatt, Ph.D. together made the difficult decision to release this secret material in the belief that knowledge is best served by being open and shared.

HEALING ENERGY, PRAYER, AND RELAXATION

Israel Regardie

Introduced by Colin Wilson

In this book Dr. Regardie sums up the essence of energized active prayer and its uses. A very important book for those interested in "enflaming thyself with prayer." This new edition contains an Appendix with three new essays by Christopher S. Hyatt, Ph.D., Joseph Lisiewski, and James Wasserman.

THE LEGEND OF ALEISTER CROWLEY

by Israel Regardie & P.R. Stephensen

This book will probably long remain as one of the most valuable and honest appraisals of the real Aleister Crowley, and can be considered factual rebuttal of the popular slander appearing in several outsider biographies.

THE EYE IN THE TRIANGLE

by Israel Regardie

Introduction by Robert Anton Wilson

"Never does Crowley make any attempt to minimize what most of us might label his worse traits in favor of the higher or more socially acceptable. It is here that is evident that magnificent difference which makes him altogether dissimilar to any other of the spiritual, metaphysical or philosophical instructors or our time." —Israel Regardie, as both student and secretary to Crowley, is eminently qualified for the task of objectively analyzing a legend.

EIGHT LECTURES ON YOGA

By Aleister Crowley

Crowley's famous Yoga for Yahoos and Yellowbellies. This is one of the best, most scientific and informative treatises on Yoga ever written. Completely dispenses with the mumbo-jumbo and focuses on the essence of the subject.

A H A

By Aleister Crowley

An epic poem incorporating Crowley's aspirations, ideals and achievements relative to magick and mysticism.

LITTLE ESSAYS TOWARD TRUTH

By Aleister Crowley

These lucid writings are some of Crowley's clearest thought on numerous qabalistic and philosophical issues among which are Man, Memory, Sorrow, Wonder, Beatitude, Laughter, Mastery, Trance, Energy, Silence, Love and Truth. Includes Glossary and Diagrams.

CROWLEY ON DRUGS

By Aleister Crowley

Carefully culled from Crowley's diaries and obscure articles written under pseudonyms, as well as some of his better known writings, this collection has been edited by Hymenaus Beta, Frater Superior of the O.T.O., and includes a commentary by R. Steven Fox, a psychotherapist specializing in addiction.

FREEDOM IS A TWO-EDGED SWORD

by Jack Parsons

Edited by Cameron and Hymenaeus Beta. Oriflamme Volume One, New Series. Jack Parsons (1914-1952) was a rockets scientist, occultist and member of Agapé Lodge of Aleister Crowley's O.T.O.. His eloquent writings on the human condition and the crisis in American society convey passion, intelligence and deep conviction. "Freedom is a two-edged sword of which one edge is liberty and the other responsibility, on which both edges are exceedingly sharp; and which is not easily handled by casual, cowardly or treacherous hands. For it has been sharpened by many conflicts, tempered in many fires, quenched by much blood, and although it is always ready for the use of the courageous and high-hearted, it will not remain when the spirit that forged it is gone."

MAGICK WITHOUT TEARS

By Aleister Crowley

An annotated, unguarded personal encyclopedia of magickal instruction covering: the Qabalah; the symbols of magick; etymology and its philosophy; the major schools of magick (white, black and yellow); hints for meditation and astral projection; the tarot; astrology; the importance of talismans, lamens and pentacles; how to distinguish prophecy from coincidence; etc. Crowley at his best.

THE LAW IS FOR ALL

By Aleister Crowley

Crowley's commentary on THE BOOK OF THE LAW. It was in Cefalu, Sicily that he outdid even himself in recording his basic attitudes toward sex, love, drugs and politics, which are immortalized in this volume; edited and introduced by Israel Regardie.

THE GEMS FROM THE EQUINOX

By Aleister Crowley

A beautiful compilation of Crowley's magickal writing which first appeared in the eleven-volume EQUINOX. Selected by Dr. Israel Regardie, with his Introduction, posthumously edited by the O.T.O. for this 1989 edition. Hardbound, 1184 pages.